Professor Kohri's Travels
A Quest for Words

コオリ先生の ことば 探求紀行

著者
Authors

郡千寿子
Kohri Chizuko

多田恵実
Tada Megumi

バーマン シャーリー ジョイ
Berman, Shari Joy

コオリ先生のことば探求紀行

著者

・

郡千寿子

コオリ先生のことば探求紀行〈目次〉

第2章　ことば不思議発見

はじめに

　私たち人間の特性のひとつが「ことば」をもっていることだと言われます。ことばは、コミュニケーションになくてはならない手段のひとつですが、普段、無意識に使っている人が多いのではないでしょうか。

　インターネットや AI、ロボットや宇宙ロケットの開発など科学技術の革新はすさまじい勢いで進んでいます。医療や医薬分野の研究も飛躍的に進歩を遂げ、新しい治療法も開発されてきました。その一方で、毎日使っている母語の日本語について、私たちはいったいどれほど理解しているでしょうか。意外にも知らないことが多く、その謎の解明に日々挑み続けているのが、私を含めた日本語学の研究者たちです。

　近年、社会にすぐ役に立つ学問研究が重要視され、有益性が見えにくい文学や言語、芸術といった研究分野の存在意義が問われています。しかし、人類誕生以来、変わらない課題はいかに生きるかということではないでしょうか。人として生まれ、愛され、愛し、喜び、悲しみ、悩みながら成熟し、老いて死を迎える…。先進諸国であろうと発展途上国であろうと、いつの時代であっても人として生きていく営みに変わりはありません。文学や芸術は、個々の人々の感性を豊かにし、想像力や創造力を養い、良き人生を送るために影響を与え得るものと確信しています。

　心身疲弊している時、話を聞いてもらい、ことばを交わすうちに癒されたり励まされたりした経験はないでしょうか。反対に心ないことばを投げかけられて傷ついた経験はないでしょうか。ことばは力をもっています。人を勇気づけもしますが、貶めもするもの…。毎日使っている日本語の本質を知り、その作用や魅力について感じてほしいと願っています。

　日本語について知ることは、日本や日本人について考えることにもつながります。他国から日本に留学中の学生さんや他国在住で日本に興味をもって下さっている人たちにも読んでほしいとの思いから、後半は英語版になっています。多田恵実先生とバーマン シャーリー ジョイ先生の献身的なご尽力のおかげで英語版を作成することができました。ディスカッションしながら日本語を母語としない読者にも理解しやすく読みやすいことを第一に考えた英訳をこころがけました。

また英語版には、日本語の理解とともに日本の古典文学や歴史についても学ぶことができるように注釈を付しました。

　日本語と英語で紡いだ、ことばを巡る探求の旅…。好奇心の種が身近なことばにも潜んでいることに気づき、あれこれと空想し思考する楽しさを一緒に感じていただきたいと思っています。ありふれたことばひとつひとつに不思議で多彩な物語がある、そして使い手の心がことばに表れる、とお伝えすることができれば幸いです。

　本書の第1章は「コオリ先生のことば探求紀行」と題して2021年9月〜2022年8月の一年間『東奥日報』（青森県）文化欄に連載したエッセイが基となっています。氏名を冠した題名は新聞社のご指示でしたが、担当者が付けて下さった各エッセイの見出しも使わせていただきました。イラストは、当時、弘前大学の大学院生だった、つちや牧子さんが担当下さいました。第2章「ことば不思議発見」は、時事通信社（東京）文化部からの依頼で助教授時代に執筆した連載です。ことばに関するコラムを中学生にもわかるように書いてほしいとの要請で全国の地方新聞に配信されました。第1章は青森県在住の読者を意識して地域色を盛り込んだ内容となっています。第2章は字数の関係で要点を絞った文体で記しています。当時のイラスト担当者に連絡がとれないという事情で新たにつちやさんが挿絵を描いて下さいました。新聞連載という性格上、掲載時の時節やトピックを取り上げているため、現時点との不整合がありますが、原文を尊重したことをご理解下さい。

　最後になりましたが、東奥日報社、時事通信社には連載原稿の出版を快諾いただき、関係者各位にこの場を借りて御礼申し上げます。刊行にあたって弘前大学出版会編集長の柏木明子先生、佐藤光輝先生、岩井草介先生はじめ教職員の方々に大変お世話になりました。また原稿執筆に際し、個々に記していませんが、先人による研究成果の蓄積の数々を参考とさせていただきました。

　多くの方々のご助力ご支援によって本書の刊行が叶いましたことに心より感謝申し上げます。

2023年錦秋

郡　千寿子

第 1 章

コオリ先生のことば探求紀行

1 日本の国語 —日本語—
過去を知り未来見据える

　世界には 3000 〜 6000 の言語が存在するといわれています。日本には日本人が住み、そのほとんどが日本語を話している。当たり前のこうした言語環境は世界では少数派です。

　2021 年のＮＨＫ大河ドラマ「青天を衝け」の主人公は実業家の渋沢栄一で、彼の生き様や思想に今あらためて注目が集まっています。2024 年発行の新一万円紙幣には渋沢の肖像が印刷されますが、日本の紙幣は「壱万円」「YEN」と漢字と英語で表示されています。

　他方、インド紙幣の表面は国語のヒンディー語と英語が、裏面はベンガル語、タミル語、アッサム語など 15 の言語が表示され、インドが多言語の国であることを物語っています。スイスは、ドイツ語使用者が最多ですが、フランス語、イタリア語、ロマンシュ語の 4 言語が国語。このように一つの国に複数の言語が存在することは珍しいことではありません。

　ところで、渋沢が活躍した明治維新以降、日本の国語が問題視されたことがありました。開国し欧米と対等に交易する際、日本語の難解さが障害と考えた初代文部大臣の森有礼は、英語

の国語化を提唱しました。文豪の志賀直哉はフランス語を推奨。もし、日本語廃止が政治的に決定されたなら、家族とは津軽弁や南部弁で話す一方、学校の授業や会話など、公用はすべて英語で、という日常生活を送るようになっていた可能性があります。

　日本語がこれからどうなっていくのか。それは使い手である私たちの考え方に左右され、使い方にゆだねられています。過去を知ることは現在について考え、未来を見据えることにつながっているのです。

　移動が制限され、人との交流が妨げられたコロナ禍…。効率的で有益なものだけでなく、一見無駄に思える何気ない雑談やゆとりの時間が、かけがえないものだと気づいた方も多いのではないでしょうか。技術革新や科学的な情報はもちろん重要ですが、どんな方針をとるかは、哲学や倫理といった人文社会学の知見も必要不可欠。

　身近なことばについて知り、ことばの使い方を考えることも決して無意味ではありません。私は鎌倉室町期から江戸時代の古い文献資料から、日本語の変遷過程の解明に挑んでいる研究者です。普段、無意識に使っていることばの不思議について一緒に考えてみませんか。

（注）コロナ禍は、新型コロナ感染症が流行した 2020 年 1 月〜 2022 年 12 月頃の約 3 年間を指す。

2 「べんとう」をめぐって
フランスで定着　日常語に

　新型コロナ感染症の拡大防止のため、外食にも行かず、昼休みは毎日持参した手作り弁当をひとりで食べています。さて今日のテーマはその「べんとう」。

　日本語としての「べんとう」が文献に表れるのは室町時代のこと。儒教の経典の講義記録『周易抄』（1477年）に「右は便当に事をするぞ」とあって「便利なこと」「都合がよいこと」を意味することばでした。中国語起源で漢字表記は「便当」が使われ、現在の日本語の「べんとう」とは違う意味を担っていたのです。

　17世紀初頭、日本語学習のためにイエズス会の宣教師たちが刊行した『日葡辞書』（1603年）には「ベンタウ」の項に「豊富、十分」に加えて「弁当箱」の意味が記載されています。つまり、中国の漢語「便当」が「便利なもの」という意味から派生し、日本で新たに「携行食」という意味でも使われるようになったことを物語っています。私がランチで持参する「弁当」は「弁当や花見の種をまくの内」と俳諧（1665年）にあるように江戸時代に一般化したものです。

　一気に21世紀現在の話

題に飛びますが、娘とフランスのパリを散策していた時のこと。私は街角のウインドーに書かれた面白い文字を見つけました。「bento」この英語、いえいえ実は「ベントー」と読む、れっきとした「フランス語」です。健康志向と相まってフランスで流行している「bento」。色とりどりの具材が一つの器に美しく詰められた、栄養豊富で便利な日本の弁当がその発祥ルーツです。

　フランスで2013年に刊行された辞書には「bento」が立項されていて「持参して昼休みに食べる食事　日本語由来」と解説されています。辞書にどのことばを掲載するかは編集者次第ですが、辞書に立項されているということはフランスですっかり定着して日常語となった証です。日本語からフランス語になったことばは「haiku（俳句）」「kimono（着物）」などがすでに1990年刊行の辞書に掲載されています。

　「便当」から「弁当」、そしてフランス語「bento」へ…。ことばを巡る探究紀行。江戸時代から日本で受け継がれた弁当文化が、今や遠くフランスのパリジェンヌ達をも魅了しています。なんとも誇らしいことではありませんか！

3 「やさしい」をめぐって
評価の褒めことばへ発展

　新型コロナ感染拡大の渦中、2020 年 4 月に第 14 代学長に就任された福田眞作先生は、消化器内科学がご専門の医学博士です。「日本一、学生に優しい大学をつくる！」と宣言され、ワクチン職域接種をはじめ強力なリーダーシップで大学運営を牽引されています。

　弘前大学は学生が学びやすく相談しやすい環境づくりや経済支援に力を注いでいますが、コロナ禍の現在、困窮する学生に対し、地域の皆様からもご寄付や様々なご支援を頂戴しています。この場を借りて心より感謝申し上げます。学生自身も受けたご恩を忘れず、周囲を思い遣れる優しい人に成長してほしいと願いながら、私も日々の教育に携わっています。

　その「やさしい」の古語「やさし」は動詞「痩す」と同根です。「やさしい」が「痩せる」に通じているとは不思議ですよね。『万葉集』に「思ひやす」という語が出てきます。現在でも「痩せる思いをする」という表現があるように、気を遣い過ぎて身の細ることも「痩す」と言いました。

　「世間を憂しとやさしと思へども飛び立ちかねつ鳥にしあらねば」（『万葉集』巻 5）は「今の世は、憂鬱で身も痩せるように辛いけれど、飛び去って逃げるわけにはいかないなあ、私は鳥ではないのだから」という悲嘆の和歌。平安時代初期に成立した『日本霊異記』の「嗚呼、恥かしきかな、やさしきかな」に見られるように「やさし」は、痩せる気持ちがするほど「恥ずかしい」気持ちも表しました。

　身が痩せるほど細やかな心遣いや恥じ入る姿態は、周囲や相手か

ら見た場合、気持ち魅かれる美しさと映るようになり、称讃されるようになっていきます。自分の感情を表すことばの「やさし」が、平安の貴族社会で次第に客観的にみた、評価の褒めことばへと発展し今に至るのです。「容易」という別の意の「易しい」の方は、江戸時代末期に新しく使い始められたものです。

　本学ゆかりの太宰治が、河盛好蔵氏宛の手紙に記しています。「この字をよく見ると、人偏に憂ふると書いてゐます。人を憂へる、ひとの淋しさ侘しさ、つらさに敏感な事、これが優しさであり、また人間として一番優れてゐる事ぢやないかしら、さうして、そんな、やさしい人の表情は、いつでも含羞であります。」繊細な心をもつ照れ屋の太宰らしい解釈ですが、彼も「優しい」を重視していたようです。

4 | ミステリーの言語学
研究は小説より奇なり

　読書の秋なので本の話題を…。国鉄蒲田操車場構内で扼殺死体が発見された。被害者の身元が判らず捜査は難航。刑事たちは、事件前夜に被害者と酒を飲んでいた若い男の存在に行き当たる。東北訛りの「カメダ」ということばを数少ない手がかりに男の行方を追う…。松本清張の『砂の器』は、東北弁が事件解決のカギとなる社会派推理小説。実在の国立国語研究所の研究者が「方言周圏論」を刑事に教授することから、事件の意外な背景が判明していきます。

　森村誠一の『人間の証明』は、西条八十詩集と麦わら帽子がキーワード。被害者が死の間際に発した「ストウハ」「キスミー」の謎とは？英語の初学者がr音を弱く発音することに由来するようで、言語学者の証言を糸口に捜査が進展します。このように小説の世界でも言語学の研究成果が科学的根拠となる事例は多く、社会に貢献し得る分野なのです。

　ミステリーに夢中だった小学生の頃。寝食忘れて没頭し、コナン・ドイルやアガサ・クリスティーなどの海外作品も読破。トリックよりも、子どもながらに描かれた人間社会の悲哀や理不尽さに興味を惹かれました。本を通して未知の世界に触れ、感受性や想像力が養われたように思います。

　推理小説は、謎を解く過程を楽しむもの。証拠をひとつひとつ積み上げて論理的に思考し犯人に迫っていく。結論がわからず、解決までの紆余曲折をドキドキしながらたどる道筋は、研究に似ているのではないか…。ことばの現象を詳細に観察し、証拠を集め、仮説を立て考

察検討していく。謎が新たな謎を呼ぶことも日常茶飯事。飽くなき好奇心と粘り強さが研究者に求められる資質です。推理小説同様、読者を納得させる論証ができなければ、研究成果は認められません。今は情報も解答案も安易に得られる時代。でも自身で悶々と悩む時間や迷う経験があってこそ得られる充実感や達成感があるのではないでしょうか。

　ところで、一般に東北弁と一括りにされますが、地域住民にとっては一様でなく、青森と秋田は違う、青森県内でも津軽と南部は違うとの意見があることでしょう。関西弁も、大阪と京都は違いますし、神戸も独特の表現が存在します。前述の『砂の器』の東北弁の正体ですが、推理小説の種あかしはご法度。気になる方は、秋の夜長にご一読下さいね。

(注)『人間の証明』ではr音について「スペイン語系を隠そうと意識的にr音を弱く発音する場合がある」と記載されているが、バーマン先生からの助言によって修正した。

5 | 科学と日本語
母語で学び考える力育む

　真鍋淑郎氏がノーベル物理学賞を受賞され、研究成果の素晴らしさやお人柄に注目が集まっています。基礎研究が認められるまでには長い年月を必要としますが、90歳の現在も好奇心と探究心に突き動かされて研究に邁進されている生き様に胸を打たれました。

　弘前大学でも世界トップレベルの研究者を招いた学術講演会を開催し、人類学者の山極壽一氏が「サル化する人間社会」、ノーベル化学賞受賞者の白川英樹氏が「科学を学ぶ－日本語と英語－」、ノーベル物理学賞受賞者の天野浩氏が「世界を照らすLED」、日本文学者のロバート　キャンベル氏が「翻訳で初めて見えてくる日本」、ノーベル生理学医学賞受賞者の本庶佑氏が「獲得免疫の驚くべき幸運」と題して講演下さいました。数多くの失敗や試行錯誤の経験がその後の新発見につながったこと、幸運は果てしなき地道な努力の先にあるなど、一流の先生方の熱意と魅力あふれる言動に触れる機会は多くの学びと刺激に満ちた時間でした。

　白川英樹先生のお話は日本の初等教育を考える上で示唆に富むものです。外国人特派員からの問い「ノーベル賞受賞がアジア諸国の中で日本人が際立って多いのはなぜか」がずっと気になっていた白川先生。導き出した答えが「科学を日本語で学ぶことができたおかげ」。諸外国では英語で科学を学ぶが日本では母語の日本語で学ぶ。言語は単に伝達の道具というだけでなく思考の道具である。考える根底に日本語がある。英語は世界に発信し交流するために必要だが日本語でしっかり考える力を育むことが大切…。国際派の数学者、藤原正彦氏も『祖

国とは国語』で国語教育の重要性に言及し、論理を育み情緒を培い、すべての知的活動の源が国語力だと説いています。

　「科学」は明治期に日本で新たに作られたことば。文明開化によって急激に流入した西洋の概念はそれまでの日本にはありません。そのため漢字を利用した新しいことばを模索し造語したのです。

　science をどう表現するか。1881 年の『哲学字彙』が初出で一般に普及するのは明治末期以降。chemistry は川本幸民が 1860 年に「化学」と翻訳します。新しい思想や制度を吸収し、日本語化しようと格闘した明治の先人たちのおかげで、「科学」をはじめ「個人」「社会」「会社」「銀行」「哲学」「自由」「主義」等々の新語が誕生し定着したのです。

6 | 「方言」への意識
残すべき大切な文化遺産

　弘前では「津軽のことばは好き。でも恥ずかしい」と矛盾した意識をもつ割合が高いとの調査報告があります。「あずましい」「しばれる」など学生たちに教えてもらった方言には何とも言えない温かさや純朴さがあって、私も大好きになりました。ことばの多様性は、表現やコミュニケーションの豊かさを支えていると言えるでしょう。

　私の故郷奈良は、地域のことばに無関心な人が多い印象です。実家の父と妹は毎日大阪へ通勤通学、私も奈良県外の大学へといった具合に県内で生活が完結しません。先祖代々奈良にお住まいの方は地元への愛着が強いかもしれませんが、京都大阪のベッドタウン滋賀県や首都圏の千葉県も同様の調査結果が出ていて居住地のことばに関心が低い地域です。

　「方言」の語は、平安時代初期の『東大寺諷誦文稿（とうだいじふじゅもんこう）』に「此当国方言毛人方言飛騨方言東国方言」と見られ、古くからことばの地域差が認識されていました。「東国方言」とあるように、今は関東のことばが共通語と思われていますが、昔は地方語の扱いだったのです。都が置かれた関西、特に京都の貴族社会のことば

が基準とされたことが文献資料から読み取れます。『源氏物語』では常陸介やその従者が「いやしきあづま声」と蔑まれています。『今昔物語集』でも「東国語は東鳥が鳴き合ひたる様」とけなされ、『平家物語』でも木曽義仲の言動が揶揄されるなど、地方が低く見られていたことがうかがえます。

　明治期以降、教育政策で標準語が推奨されたこともあって方言が重要視されない時代が長く続いてきました。しかし、地方のことばが失われつつある現在、方言は残すべき大切な文化遺産としてその価値が認められるようになっています。ことばは意識的に受け継いでいかなければ、残す努力をしなければ消滅してしまう。

　弘前大学では、人工知能 AI を使って津軽弁を共通語に自動翻訳する研究をすすめていて、研究者は今も津軽弁の個性と格闘中です。また、方言を扱う授業では学生が、主体的に学び合い活気に満ちた時間となっています。共通語圏の札幌や東京出身の学生にとっても地域特性や歴史背景を考えるきっかけとなり、有意義な学びにつながっているようです。本学の教養教育は総合大学の利点を生かし、方言に限らず、地域課題をテーマに多元的な視点や思考法の獲得を目指す教育を展開しています。

7 「そば」をめぐって
食糧難救い世界で活躍

　青森鰺ヶ沢で「ニシンそば」のメニューを見て驚いた私…。京都名物なので京都の蕎麦屋にしかないと思い込んでいました。北海道から若狭小浜を経由して運ばれた身欠ニシンを甘露煮にし蕎麦にトッピングしたニシンそば。江戸時代の北前船がルーツという歴史背景を考えれば、東北日本海沿岸の鰺ヶ沢で供されることも納得です。そういえば大阪名物の塩昆布も北前船が運んだ北海道の昆布を加工したもの。関西食文化の一端は、北前船の日本海交易による恩恵で培われたものなのですね。

　一方ソバの方ですが、文献に現れるのは古く『続日本紀』の養老6年に元正天皇が飢饉に備えて栽培を勧めた記載があり、平安時代の辞書『倭名類聚抄』に「曽波牟岐」「久呂無木」と見えます。橘成

季が編んだ説話集『古今著聞集』（1254年）には、道明阿闍梨が山人にソバムギを出され「鳥さえ食べないソバだが意外に美味しい」と感心する話が掲載されています。まだ一般的な食用でなかったようですが、鎌倉時代以降、高野山や東大寺の僧が「そばかい餅」を作った記録が散見さ

れるようになります。『宇治拾遺物語』にも比叡山延暦寺の小僧が、かい餅の出来上がりを狸寝入りしながら楽しみに待つ話があります。寝入っている小僧を起こすのはかわいそうだと放置されて結局食べ損ねてしまうのですが、ソバ粉を湯で練った「そばがき」として食したようです。

　飢饉対策としての非常食から日常食となるのは江戸時代中期のこと。生産地の信州や北関東からの供給もあり、百万都市江戸の食を支えました。蕎麦屋が繁盛し、そば切りという麺の形状で庶民に食されるようになります。『本草書』に体に良いと記載され、年越し蕎麦の風習も広まっていきました。

　「津軽そば」は大豆の汁でそば粉を練って一晩おいて作るそうですが、『蕎麦全書』（1751年）に同様の作り方が載っています。私の好きな天ぷら蕎麦は、幕末の『守貞漫稿』に「芝海老の油あげ三、四を加ふ」と登場。福島・会津の辛み大根の絞り汁で食べる蕎麦など地域による特色があって多彩です。

　日本に限らずフランスでは、そば粉のガレットが人気。北イタリアのピッゾケッリはそば粉のパスタ。ロシアや中国でも食され、ドイツではそば粉をソーセージのつなぎに使うこともあるとか…。各地の食糧難を救い、様々な工夫で受け継がれてきたのですね。

8 乾杯の挨拶
中国語起源　定着例多く

　忘年会や新年会の宴席に付きものの「乾杯の挨拶」。立場上、依頼されることがありますが、「乾杯」も「挨拶」も日本に古くから存在したことばではなく、中国語が起源の漢語です。「乾杯」と表記され、祝杯をあげる意味で使われたのは大正時代以降と最近のこと。水上滝太郎『大阪の宿』（1925年）に「廃業を祝して乾杯」とありますが、以前の日本では「乾く」ではなく「勧める」という漢字を使っていたようです。平安時代の古辞書『色葉字類抄』や『易林本節用集』（1597年）には「勧杯」とあり「乾杯」は掲載されていません。

　中国で開催された国際学会の懇親会でのこと…。中国人の研究者から「郡先生、かんぱいは杯を乾かすのだから、グイッと飲みきって下さい！」と言われて下戸の私は青くなりました。中国では文字通り杯を乾かす、飲み干すことなのですね。コロナ禍の今、宴席は自粛していますが、座を白けさせないために、杯に水を満たして素知らぬ顔でグイッと飲み干すという工夫をしていたことがあります。

　「あいさつ」の語も今やすっかり日本語に溶け込んでいますが、本来は中国語起源の仏教用語。「挨」も「拶」も「押す」という意味で、原義は「前にあるものをおしのけて進み出す」。禅宗の禅問答で「その力量を測る」意味に「挨拶」の語が使われるようになり、その後、ことばのやりとりを指すように変化したのです。

　仏教の用語が日本に入って定着する例は多く、「蒲団」や「旦那」もその仲間です。禅問答が発祥の「挨拶」は双方真剣に対峙して力量を推し量ること。つまり挨拶は人柄や能力を表すことでもあるのです。

このように本来の意味を知っていれば、挨拶がいかに大切なもので、おろそかにできないかがわかるでしょう。

　政治家が懇親会の席上で語った内容が取り沙汰され、問題に発展する事例がありますが、どのような態度で、どういう思想なのか、その人の資質や能力が問われるのが挨拶です。聴衆である受け手も、本音なのか取り繕われたものかを見極める鑑識眼が必要です。挨拶ひとつで尊敬を集めることもあれば、信用を失墜することも…。かく言う私も挨拶は得意ではありませんが、せめて人間性を磨く努力を心がけたいと思っています。

　年の瀬となりました。拙稿をお読み下さっていることに感謝しつつ皆様の一年を慰労申し上げます。どうか良いお年をお迎え下さい。

9 わが家のお雑煮
方言と食文化に共通項

　新年あけましておめでとうございます。お正月、皆様はどんなお雑煮を召し上がりましたか？　新年を「雑煮」で祝う風習は室町時代末期に起こりました。1603年の『日葡辞書』に「Zoni ザウニ（雑煮）正月に出される餅と野菜とで作った食物の一種」と説明され、『料理物語』（1643年）には「雑煮はみそ又すましにても仕立候。もち、とうふ、いも、大こん、いりこ、くしあわび、ひしがつほ、くきたちなど入よし」とあります。主役の餅が丸いか四角いか、味噌かすましか、地域や家庭ごとの調理法や具材に特徴があり、まさしく日本の食文化の伝統と個性が象徴されていると言えるでしょう。

　わが家は昆布と鰹のすまし汁に鶏肉、かまぼこ、三つ葉、ゆずを入れたシンプルな雑煮。焼いた四角い切り餅を入れます。東京出身の母からの継承で関東風雑煮です。奈良出身の伯母宅（郡家の本家）では、里芋、大根、人参にお豆腐、鶏肉の具材に赤白の合わせ味噌で調理して、丸餅を焼いて入れます。このお餅、食べる時に甘いきな粉をつけて食べるそうです。雑煮ときな粉の取合わせにびっくりです。青森出身の大学秘書さん宅の雑煮は、根菜やせりといった野菜に高野豆腐が入ったしょうゆ風味のだし汁に角餅を入れて煮る、と教えていただきました。

　『日本の食生活全集（全50巻）』（農村漁村文化協会刊）で調べてみると東海から関東、中部にかけて東日本は角餅で、近畿から中国、四国、九州は丸餅と二分化しています。面白いことに味噌を使うのは近畿、福井、四国の香川、徳島に限られていて、関東を含め圧倒的多数

がすましの地域でした。石川の能登、鳥取、島根の出雲には小豆を使っ
た雑煮があるようです。餅の形状では、日本海側は角餅の富山と丸餅
の石川間、太平洋側は角餅の三重と丸餅の滋賀間に境界線が引けそう
です。私が熟知している方言の東西分岐ラインに類似しています。食
文化もことばも、継承されながら長い時間をかけて変化していくため、
形成過程の背景要因には共通項があるのかもしれません。

　友人宅では元旦に妻の関西風、翌二日は夫の関東風と双方を尊重し
た異文化交流が実践されています。祝い椀の雑煮を巡る伝統や地域性
に思いを馳せながら、家族や故郷を思うお正月。気持ち新たに素敵な
年となりますよう皆様のご多幸をお祈り申し上げます。今年もどうか
よろしくお願いいたします。

10 うまい or おいしい
女性の柔軟な発想　新語に

　味の良い料理を食した時、思わず発することば「うまい」と「おいしい」…。皆さんはどちらを使いますか？　女性は「おいしい」を使うと思っていた私は、とある女子学生が「うまい！」と言った場面に遭遇してびっくり。でも以前から青森では「うまい」が標準形だったようです。

　1965年頃の方言調査『日本言語地図』（国立国語研究所）によれば、関西地方や北陸の一部で「OISII（おいしい）」が使われていますが、九州は「NMAKA（んまか）」、岩手と秋田は「NME（んめ）」、関東と青森は「UMAI（うまい）」であることが確認できます。

　近年刊行された『日本語語感の辞典』には「おいしい」が「味がよい意の上品な表現だったが今では男性も多用するようになり、普通のことばに近づきつつある」と説明されています。一部の人が使う特別な表現が多くの人に使われるうちに一般的なことばになる…。このような現象は他にも見られ、多用されるうちに敬意度が下がることを「敬意低減の法則」と呼びます。たとえば「お母さん」も当初は尊敬の気持ちを有した尊敬表現でしたが、次第に一般の呼称になった例と言えます。

　さて「おいしい」ですが、関西地方が発祥でそれが周囲に広がったと推測できます。もっと遡れば、今は聞き慣れない「いしい」ということばでした。室町期の言語を反映している『日葡辞書』に「いしい」と立項され「婦人語」と解説されています。江戸時代の女子向けの作法書『女寺子調法記』にも女性が「うまいをいしゐ」と言い換えたこ

とが記されています。使う女性が増えるにつれて品位が下がり、丁寧の接頭語「お」が冠された「おいしい」が使われ始めて定着。幕末、宣教師として来日したヘボン編纂の『和英語林集成』には「おいしい」で立項され「女性語」とあります。長く「いしい」「おいしい」が女性のことばと認識されていたことが知られます。

　丁寧なことば遣いをしようと考えた男性たちもまねるようになって普及し、半世紀以上の時間をかけて使用者も地域も拡大していったのですね。女性が柔軟な発想で新語を生み出し流行させ、周囲の男性や社会に影響を及ぼす…。そうした経緯で今に至ることばは「おいしい」だけではありません。ことばのバトンを繋ぎ続けた女性達の活躍を日本語の歴史の中にも見ることができるのです。

11 | ちずこ or ちづこ
発音と文字表記　並進せず

　先月のある日「お誕生日おめでとうございます！」と花束を頂戴しました。私の誕生日を気にかけてくれていた同僚職員に感謝感激。関西では珍しく雪の舞う寒い日に生まれた私。この世に生を受け最初のプレゼントが名前と言われますが、「千寿子」という命名には、両親の願いが込められています。ひらがなでは「ちずこ」ですが、時々「ちづこ」と間違えられます。「千寿子」も「千鶴子」も「千津子」も、聞き分けることができないため、漢字が添えられないと「ず」か「づ」かの区別ができず混乱する人が多いのですね。どうして発音が同じなのにひらがな文字は二つ存在しているのでしょうか。

　「水」は現代の辞書では「みず」とひらがな表記されています。しかし古くは「みづ」だったのです。平安時代の辞書『色葉字類抄』では漢字「水」に「ミヅ」と付訓されています。1251年成立『観智院本類聚名義抄』、1474年成立『文明本節用集』、1717年成立『書言字考節用集』でも「水」は「ミヅ」と記載されているのです。

　1577年に来日したポルトガル人のロドリゲス。彼は外国人宣教師の日本語学

習のために『日本語文典』という文法書を編集するほどの日本語通です。その彼が当時の日本の人々のことば遣いを「水をミズ、参らずをマイラヅと発音することがある」と語っています。つまり、本来ミヅと発音すべきなのにミズと誤って発音する人やマイラズが正しいのにマイラヅと発音する人がいると言うのです。違う別の発音であるはずの「ズ」と「ヅ」が当時、混同されつつある状況だったことを物語っています。「水」は古く〔midu〕と発音され〔midzu〕を経て次第に〔mizu〕へと変化し定着します。江戸時代の文献によれば、発音が変化したにもかかわらず仮名表記は追随せず、古形を継承したことが知られます。「ズ」と「ヅ」に加えて「ジ」「ヂ」も同様の歴史を辿って今に至ります。ひらがな文字の違いは発音の違いでもあったのです。他方ワ行の「ゐ」と「ゑ」は、発音がア行「イ」「エ」に集約されたことに伴ってひらがな文字が消滅します。こちらは明治期以降に国語政策として人為的に整備された結果です。

　日本語の変わりゆく姿をどのように受け入れるか。発音の変化と文字表記の変化が同時進行でなかったことによる混乱の一端が「ちずこ」と「ちづこ」に現れているとも言えそうです。

12 | 梅の花見
知識人らの教養力試す場

　日本各地で梅の開花が報じられる季節となりました。『万葉集』巻
５の「梅の花見」は元号「令和」の出典箇所。「梅花歌三十二首并序
天平二年正月十三日　萃帥老之宅　申宴会也　于時初春令月　気淑風
和　梅披鏡前之粉　蘭薫珮後之香」。王羲之の蘭亭序などの初唐詩の
序の構成や語句を倣っていると言われるところです。天平２年（730
年）正月十三日に大伴旅人宅に集まって宴会が催された。時折しも初
春の佳き月、空気は美しく風は穏やかで、梅の花は鏡の前に装う美女
の白粉のごとく咲き誇り、香草は匂い袋のように薫りたっていた…。

　平城京、奈良の都から遠く離れた田舎の大宰府に赴任している官僚
たちが、花見の宴会をして和歌を詠む場面です。花見といえば現在で
は桜ですが、当時、梅は舶来の輸入植物で貴族の家の庭にしかなかっ
たのです。ですから梅の花を見ながらの宴会はハイカラな催しでした。
太宰府には筑紫の国守として山上憶良が726年頃赴任し、その１〜２
年後に大伴旅人が妻の大伴郎女を伴って赴任しています。大宰府は朝
鮮半島や中国大陸に近く、国際、文化交流という点では最先端の地で
した。そしてこの宴会は単なる酒宴や花見を楽しむことが目的なので
はなく、知識人たちの教養力が試される、学力や知力の戦いの場でも
あったのです。

　『万葉集』には160種類以上の植物が登場し、古の人がいかに植物
を身近に感じていたかがうかがえます。犬養孝著『万葉のいぶき』（新
潮文庫）によれば、『万葉集』に最も多く詠まれた植物は萩で140首、
次いで梅が118首、桜は意外に少なく40首。春の花見では梅が、秋

の花見では萩が詠まれ、桜より梅が圧倒的に多く登場することから、古代は「花」といえば桜でなく梅だったと言われます。しかし中西進先生（令和の考案者）によれば、この5巻のように梅に限った和歌が詠まれる場面が『万葉集』に多いという特性からであって、当時も桜は花の代表格だったのではないかとおっしゃっています。

　弘前在住の私としては桜の花見も推奨したいところ。平安時代の古典では桜の登場が多くなり、『枕草子』では梅12に対し桜29、『源氏物語』では梅34に対し桜53と逆転します（宮島達夫編『古典対照語い表』笠間書院による）。青森では、五所川原の北限の梅祭りが4月下旬頃。桜の開花とほぼ同じ時期に梅の花も楽しめるとは何ともぜいたくな地域と言えるかもしれません。

13 桃の節句
邪気払い　成長祈る果樹

　３月３日はひな祭り、桃の節句。桃は梅や桜と同じバラ科の植物です。本連載の編集担当の方はご子息に「桃太郎」と命名されたこともあって桃に強い思い入れがあるそうです。私のゼミ生にも「桃太郎」という青森出身の好青年がいます。卒業後は千葉の小学校教師となり、結婚式にも参列した思い出深い教え子のひとりです。ご両親が心優しくも勇敢な「昔話の桃太郎」にちなんで命名されたそうです。

　ひな祭りは、古代中国で３月最初の巳（み）の日に行われる「上巳節（じょうしせつ）」が平安時代に日本に入り、室町時代の貴族の女児達の人形遊び「ひいな祭り」と融合してできたと言われます。江戸時代に五節句の一つとして制度化され一般民衆にも広まりました。

　桃の花が雛段（ひな）に供えられるのには理由があります。古くから中国では桃は邪気を払う霊力があると信じられ、『春秋左氏伝』に桃の木で作った弓が災いを払うと記述があります。日本でも『古事記』の国生み神話で伊弉諾尊（いざなきのみこと）が黄泉（よみ）の国から逃走する際に追っ手に桃の実を投げて彼らを追い払う場面が出てきます。昔から、桃の実や枝が邪気を払う植物であったことが知られます。鬼を退治する昔話の桃太郎が、他の果樹でなく桃から生まれたことには必然性があったのですね。

　ひな祭りに桃の枝を飾るのも、悪い者から女児を守り、無事の成長を祈るという意味が込められていたのでしょう。中国では不老長寿を象徴する樹木であるともされ、陶淵明『桃花源記（とうえんめい）』に見られる桃源境伝説が有名です。

　式亭三馬の書き入れがある赤本『桃太郎』は、おなじみの「むかし

むかし、爺は山へ柴刈りに婆は川へ洗濯に行き」で始まりますが、婆が川に流れてきた桃を取って家に帰り、この桃を食べた夫婦が若返って子どもを授かるという話。桃太郎と名付けられ鬼退治に行くのは同様ですが、よく知られた大きな桃から子どもが誕生する類型とは違う物語が江戸時代には存在しました。

　梅や桜は和歌に多く詠まれます。一方桃は漢詩文でよく詠まれました。『源氏物語』『古今和歌集』では梅と桜は登場回数が多いですが桃は一度も見られません。観賞の対象だった梅と桜に比して桃は違った役割を担っていたようです。

　農林水産省の作物調査（2021年）によれば桃の生産量は山梨が31％を占め一位。福島、長野、山形、和歌山と続きます。桃太郎伝説の吉備の国、岡山が上位に入っていないのは意外でした。

14 善知鳥神社の思い出
悲話背負う地名「安方」

　卒業式など旅立ちの季節ですね。1999年3月末、まだ雪残る青森空港に不安と期待を胸に抱いて降り立った私。縁もゆかりもない青森での新生活を前に訪れた場所が、善知鳥神社でした。厳粛な気持ちで4月からの職務に精一杯取り組む決意を誓いました。不慣れな雪国で、今日まで元気に機嫌良く暮らしてこられたのは、最初に善知鳥神社にお参りしたご利益だったのかもしれない、と心細かった23年前を懐かしく思い出します。

　ウトウという鳥の棲息地は、北海道の大黒島や天売島、三陸海岸沿いの足島や椿島といった孤島で、人里ではあまりお目にかかれないようです。しかしこのウトウ、室町時代から江戸時代の終わりまで悲しい物語を背負った鳥として大変有名だったのです。謡曲『善知鳥』では次のように語られます。愚かなことにこの鳥は地面に穴を掘って卵を生む。親鳥は隠したつもりでも漁師が親鳥のまねをして「ウトウ」と呼ぶと子は「ヤスカタ」と応える。そのためすぐに漁師に見つかって取られてしまう。親鳥は悲しみのあまり空から血の涙をふりそそぐ。漁師は蓑や笠で逃れようとするが血の

涙は降り続き、あたり一面が紅（くれない）の色に染まってしまう…。

　室町時代の『鴉鷺物語（あろ）』にも「子に過ぎたる宝、さらになし。子を思ふ涙の雨の蓑の上に、うとうと鳴けば、やすかたの鳥こそ。我もまた唐紅（からくれない）の袖の露。」とあるように、ウトウの我が子を思う悲痛な心情は人々の心に響き、広く流布したのです。「陸奥（みちのく）の　外の浜なる　呼子鳥　鳴くなる声は　うとうやすかた」は、『謡曲拾葉集』に見られる古歌。謡曲や『鴉鷺物語』では、親鳥がウトウと鳴き、子がヤスカタと応えるのですが、古歌ではウトウヤスカタと鳴くことになっています。

　他方、鳥の名としてもウトウだけでなく、ウトウヤスカタが一般に使われていたようです。室町時代の辞書『運歩色葉集（うんぽいろはしゅう）』に「善知鳥悪知鳥（すかた）」「有藤安方（うとうやすかた）」「虚八姿（うとうやすかた）」と見られ、『日葡辞書』には「ウトウ」と「ヤスカタ」が鳥の名として記載されています。つまり鳴き方も鳥の名も「ウトウ」「ヤスカタ」「ウトウヤスカタ」の三種が存在し、地名の安方といつしか関連づけられたのでしょう。

　古典文学に登場する善知鳥は悲哀の象徴でした。しかし私にとっての善知鳥は、青森で最初にお参りした神社として、新天地での門出を激励してくれた懐かしい思い出として心に宿っているのです。

15 | 桜餅の不思議
青森は2種類販売　懐深く

　桜花舞う季節。和菓子屋さんには「桜餅」が並びますが地域によって材料や見た目が違うことをご存じでしょうか。

　私も編集執筆した日本最大の国語辞典『日本国語大辞典1〜13巻』（小学館）によれば、「小麦粉を水に溶いて薄く焼いた皮で餡を巻き、塩漬けにした桜の葉で包んだ菓子。」と説明されています。えっ⁉私が幼少の頃から慣れ親しんだ桜餅とは違う！「小麦粉にかえて、もち米をついたものを用いることもある。」と辞書には補足されていますが、私の思い描く「桜色の餅米をまとった桜餅」は傍流かのような説明に愕然としました。

　大学近くの行きつけの和菓子屋「こがねざわ」さんに行って確認することに…。なんと私の見慣れた餅米使用の桜餅が「道明寺」と命名されて綺麗にショーケースに鎮座しているではありませんか。そうだそうだ、傍流などでなく主流はやっぱりこの桜餅だ！と心の中で叫びました。こがねざわのご主人に「弘前ではこの桜餅が一般的ですか？」とうかがうと、「以前は二種類作って売っていましたが、もち米の道明寺の方が人気で今はこれだけにしています。弘前の他の和菓子屋さんでは小麦粉ともち米と二種類売っているお店が多いかもしれません。」とのこと…。

　『江戸名物詩』（1836年）に「長命寺桜餅」、仮名垣魯文の『胡瓜遣』（1872年）に「長命寺の山本の店（中略）桜餅の香」とあるように、江戸向島の桜の名所、長命寺門前の山本新六の考案と伝えらえているのが、小麦粉使用の皮で餡を巻いたクレープ状の桜餅。江

戸時代からずっと今も変わらずこの形状の桜餅が長命寺の名物です。これに対抗するかのように西日本エリアでは道明寺粉というもち米で餡を包んだ関西式の桜餅がいつしか誕生して普及していったようです。江戸の長命寺門前の小麦粉の方が発祥のようですが、関西生まれの私は近年まで全くその存在を知らずに育ちました。青森では関東風も関西風も両方を受け入れているそうでその懐の深さに感服です。

　西日本の中国四国、そして東海や北陸、九州ももち米桜餅が一般的なようです。山陰の一部（鳥取県西部・島根県東部）で長命寺由来の関東風が普及している地域があるそうですが、皆様はどちらがお好みでしょうか。

　桜餅を巡る歴史と地域性の不思議に思いを馳せつつ、待ちに待った春を実感しています。

16 | 新学期によせて
あらたな意味得た「新しい」

　弘前大学では 2022 年は入学式が 4 月 5 日、授業は 11 日から始まりました。4 月は一年で最も大学が活気とフレッシュな空気に満ち溢れる季節です。コロナ禍が続いていますが、各自で対策や工夫をこらし、大学生活を充実した有意義なものとしてほしいと願っています。大学に限らず、小中高校でも新学期ですね。今日は「新しい」ということばについて考えてみましょう。現代語「新しい」に連なる古語の「あたらし」をひも解くと意外な意味を有していたことが知られます。

　『古事記』に素戔嗚尊が高天原に上って来て、姉の天照大神が耕作する土地に介入し勝手な振舞をするという話があります。姉の天照大神は「田の畔を放ち、溝を埋むるは、地を阿多良斯とこそ、我がなせの命、かくしつらめ。」と言っていますが、これは、弟の傍若無人な振る舞いは土地がもったいないとの思いでやったことでしょう、との意味に解釈でき、彼を弁護している場面です。つまり「あたらし」は、土地が十分活用されていなくて残念という気持ちを表現したことばなのです。

　平安時代の『源氏物語』（梅枝）に見える「姫君の御有様、盛りに整ひて、あたらしううつくしげなり。」の一文は、そのままにしておくのは惜しいほど立派だという意味になります。「あたらし」の「あた」は「当たる」に通じ、優れたもの立派なものがそれ相応であってほしいの意味ですが、用例を検討すると、賞賛だけでなく、対象がその立派さを発揮していないときにむなしさや惜しむ気持ちを指した語であることがわかります。『万葉集』の家持の和歌では「惜しき」の漢字

表記が使われ、古語の「あたらし」は現代語「新しい」とは意味の隔たりが大きいのです。

　他方、別に「あらたし」ということばが存在します。『万葉集』に「あらたしき年の初めの初春のけふふる雪のいや重け吉事」と新春の和歌が見えますが、この「あらたし」の語が「あらたむ」「あらたまる」の類で現代につながっていきます。本来は別のことばでしたが、平安時代に「あらたし（新）」と「あたらし（可惜）」が混同されるようになり、「あたらし」は次第に「惜しむ」意味を消滅させ、本来「あらたし」が有していた「新」の意味だけを持つようになります。「あたらし」がそのまま現代語「新しい」に移行したのではなく、あらたな意味を獲得したと言えそうです。

　新学期、新しい何かがつかめる季節になればいいですね。

17 ｜ みどりの日
色の呼び方　一様でなく

　5月4日はみどりの日。新緑の季節とも言われますが、「みどり」が色彩を表すことばとして認識されるのは平安時代以降のことです。それ以前、古く万葉の頃の人々が色彩語として独立して使っていたのは、「赤」「黒」「白」「青」の4種だけでした。つまり他の多くの色はこれらで表現されていたのです。

　たとえば「あお」という語を「黄色」の意味で使う地域は今もあって方言として残存しています。『鹿角方言考』に「黄色ヲあおトイフコトアルハ誤用トイフノ外ナシ、改ムベシ」と方言是正の立場が説かれています。しかしこれは誤用ではなく、黄色という認識がなかった古の時代の呼び方が、今に受け継がれていると考えられます。秋田鹿角に限らず、沖縄や越後、飛騨など北から南の各所の方言として「黄色」を「あお」と表現する地域が確認できるのです。

　「みどり」もまた平安時代以降に「あお」から独立し色名として使われ始めたことばです。『万葉集』の「みどり児」ということばは「若々しい新芽のような未熟な子ども」という意味ですが、『万葉集』では「黄」も「緑」も色を表すことば

としては使われていません。それまで「あお」と表現していた中で、若葉のような色を指して「みどり」という色名が次第に普及していったのです。平安時代の『枕草子』には「空はみどりに霞みわたれる」「扇の骨は朴。色は赤き。紫。緑。」と色彩語としての「みどり」が確認できます。もとは「あお」が「みどり」を包括していた名残で、「赤信号」に対する「青信号」（緑色の信号）という表現に私たちはあまり不自然さを感じないのかもしれません。

　虹は7色（赤橙黄緑青藍紫）と思っていますが、これは今の日本人の色彩感覚です。古代の4種の枠組で考えれば、赤と青の2色ということも…。『日本霊異記』には「五つの色の雲あり」と虹が表現されていて5色と考えていた様子。色に対する認識や呼び方も一様ではないのですね。

　世界の言語に目を向けてみると、英語では虹は6色。アフリカ南部ジンバブエの言語の一つであるショナ語では、虹は青色で1色、緑と黄色で1色、赤と紫で1色の3色が定番。アフリカ西部のリベリアの言語の一つバサ語では、紫、青、緑がまとめて1色、黄色、橙、赤がまとめて1色の2色だとか。緑色をどう扱うかもそれぞれで面白いですね。世界は広い！

18 鳥取・境港の津軽様
「情けは人の為ならず」伝承

　私は現在、国の科学研究費で山陰地方に残存する江戸時代の文献資料を調査研究しています。山陰は東北と距離的にかなり離れていますが、不思議なつながりを感じる場所です。本書第1章4の「ミステリーの言語学」で松本清張の『砂の器』を紹介したことを覚えておられますか。東北弁を話す容疑者について「推理小説の種明かしは御法度」と解答を保留しましたが、東北弁と思われた方言は、実は出雲弁だったのです。西日本の山陰地方の一部に東北弁と似た特徴を有することばが飛び火のように存在しています。類似性の要因はわかっていませんが興味深いですよね。

　日本海域交流というテーマで山陰の文献調査を続ける私が、鳥取の境港へ出張した時のこと。当地で「津軽様」という地名を見つけて驚きました。「江戸時代後期、いつのころか小篠津村で船が難破した。船に乗っていた津軽の水主が水死し、今の花町の海岸へ漂着した。土地の人が手厚く葬ったところ、病気の者が墓参りしてお願いすると不思議とよくなった。たちまち評判となって、各地からお参りする人が続いた。津軽の人であったので「津軽様」と呼ばれた。今も台場公園の近くにある。」と『境港市史　上巻』に解説されています。

　江戸時代、北前船の寄港地であった境港は、北海道や東北からの物資を関西へ運ぶ重要な中継地点でした。海域交流の証であるかのように今も境港の一角に「津軽」の名称を冠した庶民信仰が根付いていたのです。故郷から遠く離れた地で命を落とした津軽人を哀れに思い弔ってくれた、境港の人々の情けある行動。その思いに報いるかのよ

うに巡り巡って当地の病気の人々を救うことにつながったという民間
伝承は、損得ぬきの思い遣りの大切さを伝えているかのようです。「情
けは人の為ならず」のことわざが頭をよぎりました。

　文化庁の「国語に関する世論調査」によれば「人に情けをかけるこ
とは結局はその人のためにならない」と誤解（2000年、2010年とも
に約46％が誤解）している人が多いようです。2010年の調査結果に
よれば、東北地域は他地域に比べて正答が約32％と低く、誤答が約
58％と高くなっています。正答の、他人への親切が自分にも利益をも
たらすという考え方は結果論にすぎません。後先考えずに困っている
人に手を差し伸べる姿勢をもちたいなと思います。

19 | 梅雨の季節
「つゆ」共通語　この数十年

　６月になりました。関西在住時はこの時期、湿度が高くて雨が降り続くため、憂鬱な気持ちになったものです。しかし青森では、暑くも寒くもなく、雨もそれほど多くないこの時期は、比較的過ごしやすいと感じます。「梅」と「雨」という漢字を連ねて書いて「つゆ」と読みます。このことばがこの時期特有の自然現象を指して共通認識をもたれるようになった背景について少し考えてみましょう。

　国立国語研究所編『日本言語地図６』の「つゆ（梅雨）」の方言分布をみると興味深いことがわかります。言語地図作成のための方言調査は1955年から1965年にかけて行われ、当時の使用語の実態を表しています。「ツユ」の語形は関西地方から中国地方の西日本に広く分布。一方関東周辺から東北南部では「ニューバイ」が使われています。これは「入梅」の漢字を字音読みしたものでまさしく「梅雨入り」を指した語だったと思われます。

　ほかに紀伊半島南部から東海に「ツイリ」、岩手に「ナガ（ア）メ」、四国や九州に「ナガシ」の語形が存在しています。北海道では「ツユ」と「ニューバイ」のほか一部地域で「ズリ」という珍しい語形が確認できます。「長く降り続く雨」という意味を連想させる「ナガメ」「ナガシ」系と「梅雨入り」の「ニューバイ」「ツイリ」系が次第に「ツユ」の語に合流集約されたという経緯が想定できそうです。

　共通語は、東京や関東のことばを基準にしていると思われがちですが、江戸時代まで長く都がおかれた関西のことばが、このように全国へ波及した例は少なくありません。「ツユ」も関東圏での使用歴は意

外に短く、関西圏の語形が全国へ勢力を伸ばした例と言えるでしょう。

　文献にも古く「ツイリ」「ツユ」の語が見られます。室町時代の辞書『伊京集』に「霤ツイリ」、『文明本節用集』に「雫ツユ」とあり、『易林本節用集』（1597）には「墜栗花」「霖」の漢字に「ツイリ」と見えます。「ツユ」に「梅雨」

の漢字を当てたのは1688年の『日本歳時記』の「此月淫雨ふるこれを梅雨（つゆ）と名づく」や『書言字考節用集』の「梅雨ツユ」の例がありますが、江戸時代以降に一般化したものと思われます。

　地域ごとに呼び方も違ったこの時期特有の雨が降り続く現象を「梅雨（つゆ）」と称し、全国で共通認識が図られたのはこの数十年のことだったと言えそうです。

20 桜桃忌と津軽賞
太宰文学の魅力　色あせず

　今日6月19日は、作家太宰治の誕生日で、その死が確認された日でもある「桜桃忌」。本名津島修治は、弘前大学の前身の旧制弘前高校の出身で、大学敷地内には彼ゆかりの場所がいくつか存在し、太宰の旧制高校時代の自筆ノート（英語・修身）が附属図書館に所蔵されています。複製本を本学資料館で展示していますので機会があれば参観下さい。彼の学びの様子や授業の合間の落書きなど興味深い青春の一端に触れることができるでしょう。

　弘前大学では、太宰の作品『津軽』にちなみ「太宰治記念津軽賞」を設立しました。高校生を対象にした地域探究論文コンテストで、ホームページで募集要項を公表しています。新たに学習指導要領に設けられた「総合的な探究の時間」を意識した企画で「歴史・文化・社会」「技術・環境・食」「ライフ・健康・教育」の分野別に審査を行いますが、様々な領域の研究者が揃う本学の社会貢献でもあります。多くの高校生にチャレンジしてほしい、そして「桜桃忌」のように「津軽賞」の名も全国に広まってほしいと願っているところです。

　『走れメロス』は誰もが読んだことのある最も身近な太宰作品です。なぜなら国語教科書に掲載され続けているからです。夏目漱石の『こころ』や森鴎外の『舞姫』、芥川龍之介の『羅生門』と並んで国語教科書の定番教材となっています。文豪の教科書掲載作品は長年変動がありませんが、太宰に限っては『走れメロス』のほかに『富岳百景』『女生徒』『葉桜と魔笛』『雀』『トカトントン』『待つ』『水仙』『蓄犬談』と多様な作品が採用されていることが注目されます。教育現場での魅

力や価値が今なお色あせていない証でしょう。

　評論家の亀井勝一郎は「太宰の全作品の中から、もし一つだけ選べと云はるゝなら、私は『津軽』を挙げよう。『晩年』に対する彼自ら試みた恰好の解明であり、同時に『人間失格』『斜陽』等への予言でもある。云はゞ前期と後期をつなぐ結び目のやうな作品で、太宰文学を解く最大の鍵と云つてよい。」（新潮社「太宰治集下巻」解説）と述べています。作品『津軽』は、風土記の名を借りた小説ですが、エッセイでもありルポタージュでもあり紀行文でもあり優れた地域論として読むことも可能です。

　この拙稿を書きながら太宰の小説を読み返したくなりました。

21 | 七夕
手習いの上達願う役割も

　もうすぐ「七夕」ですね。年中行事は、人々の日常生活の中で季節感を意識させるものとして大切ですが、必ずしも古い形式のまま受け継がれてきたのではなく、時代と社会の要請によって伝統を受け継ぎつつ、新しい役割を与えられて継承されてきました。

　中国の六朝時代の歳時記『荊楚歳時記』に一年に一度だけ出会う牽牛星と織女星の伝説が語られていますが、それに加えて7月7日に技の巧みになることを願う「乞巧奠」という重要な行事があったことが記されています。庭に出した台に酒や瓜、果物を供え、針に糸を通して裁縫の上達を牽牛と織女に願うのです。中国のこうした七夕伝説は早くから日本に伝えられたようで『万葉集』には130余首もの「七夕」の和歌が収載されています。

　日本では奈良時代以降、宮中で7月7日の夜に牽牛と織女の二星を祀る「乞巧奠」の儀式が節会として取り入れられました。平安時代には貴族たちによる儀礼儀式として受け継がれ優雅な風習という意味を持っていました。江戸時代になると武家の行事にも取り入れられて次第に一般庶民にも広がっていったのです。

　東北大学狩野文庫蔵『絵本天の川』には、江戸時代の人々が七夕をどう過ごしていたかが絵で描写されています。庭に設けた台に酒や瓜とともに着物や糸、琴が供えられ、笹竹に短冊が飾られている様子が確認できます。現代でも、地域によっては織女を機織りの神に見立て「七夕紙衣」という「着物をお貸しする習俗」が残っています。庶民生活の中でも、書や琴、裁縫といった手習いの上達を願う七夕は受け

継がれていたようです。七夕につきものの笹竹に短冊も見られます。今は「願いごと」を書く風習となっていますが当時は違っていました。「七夕には七夕にまつわる和歌を供える風習があるが、子供たちはどういった和歌がよいのかわからないだろうから七夕の和歌を集めて紹介する本を作った」と『七夕星歌抄』（元禄頃刊）にあり、詩歌が欠かせない要素だったのです。星に技芸の上達を願う行事である一方、子供たちが和歌を学び、書の練習を積む学習機会としての役割を担っていたのです。

　七夕は京都の貴族文化から江戸時代に地方や庶民に伝播し、子供参加型に変容することでより一層活性化し、生活に根ざした行事として定着したと言えそうです。

22 | 外来語「ビール」
蘭学者の知識と体験　発端

　盛夏を迎え、冷たいビールが恋しくなる季節。現代日本語には、この「ビール」のように外国語由来のことばが多く存在します。外国語の単語の意味と形をそのまま採り入れたことばと単純に考えられがちですが、外来語の語源や定着の背景を明らかにすることは、実は容易ではありません。身近な例でいえば、タバコはポルトガル語から、イクラはロシア語から入ってきたことば。

　飲料のビールは、缶や瓶に英語表記「BEER」が使われ、カタカナ表記「ビール」も英語由来だと誤解されがち。しかし、実はオランダ語「BIER」からの借用語なのです。飲料単独で使う場合は「ビール」ですが「hall（集会場）」と結合した場合は、「ビールホール」でなく「ビヤホール」とカタカナ表記されます。「garden（庭）」と結合した場合も、「ビールガーデン」でなく「ビヤガーデン」となりますね。あら不思議 !?　なぜでしょうか。

　「ビール」は、平戸にオランダ商館ができた 1609 年以降、オランダ人から伝わったようで、オランダ通詞が記した 1724 年成立『和蘭問答』に「ヒイルという名の麦で作られた酒は味わいも無い」と登場しています。蘭学者の大槻玄沢著『蘭説弁惑』（1799 年）には「びいる　食後に飲食の消化を助ける」とあり、福沢諭吉も『西洋衣食住』（1867 年）で「ビィールは麦酒で味は苦い」と書いています。

　蘭学者たちの知識と体験が発端となり、オランダ語「BIER」の発音が、日本に輸入され定着していったのです。日本と英語圏との交流が盛んになるにつれて英語「BEER　ビヤ」の勢力が大きくなり、外

来語と結合する場合は、英語音からの影響を受けた新語が増えていきました。しかし、和語や漢語と複合語を形成する場合は、「黒ビール」「ビール瓶」「缶ビール」「ビール工場」とオランダ語音「ビール」が消失することなく継承使用されています。

　理髪店で頭髪を刈るのに用いる器械を日本で「バリカン」と呼ぶのはなぜか。英語は「hair　clippers」、フランス語は「tondeuse」で英語やフランス語から流入したのではなさそうです。「バリカン」の由来は長く不明でしたが、金田一京助博士は初めて輸入されたこの器械が「Bariquand & Marre」という会社の製品で、その会社名が商品名となったことを発見しました。言語学者の努力と執念、そして外来語受容の不思議を物語る逸話として有名です。

23 「くだもの」をめぐって
酒の肴、菓子も同じ呼び名

　青森を代表する果物（くだもの）といえばリンゴ。ほかにも初夏のサクランボ、つがるメロン、ゼネラルクラークなどの西洋なし、収穫量日本一というカシスもありますね。青森産の果物の豊富さと美味しさに魅了されている私です。

　ところでこの「くだもの」ということば、今と昔では指し示すものが違っていました。「く」は「木」の古形で「だ」は現在の「の」という助詞に当たり、「けだもの（獣）」と同じ語構成のことばなのです。つまり「くだもの」は「木のもの（実）」という意味なのです。古辞書『和名抄（わみょうしょう）』（934年頃）に「コノミ　俗云（ぞくにいう）クダモノ」とあることからも確認できます。平安時代は、ドングリや栗（くり）といった木の実だけでなく、草の果実としてウリやナス、根の果実としてイモやレンコンも「くだもの」の仲間として扱われていました。特に草の果実は『字鏡集（じきょうしゅう）』（1245年）に「蓏　クサクダモノ」と見えるようにウリやイチゴは草果物（くさくだもの）とも呼ばれたようです。

　植物性の食品に限らず『蜻蛉日記（かげろうにっき）』（974年頃）に「その蓋に酒、くだものと入れて出す」、『観智院本類聚名義抄』に「肴　サカナ　クダモノ」と記されているように酒の肴といった副菜も「くだもの」と呼んだことが知られます。間食用の食事「菓子」を指すこともあり、『名語記（みょうごき）』（1275年）に「くだもの如何。菓子とかけり」とあります。

　木の実や酒の肴、菓子をも指した「くだもの」が現代語のようにもっぱら果実の意となるのは江戸時代中期頃のことです。くだものと同義語だった「菓子」の方は、大陸との交流や茶の湯の発達によって

饅頭などの甘い菓子が登場し、次第に現代の意に限定されていきます。果実のくだものは「水菓子」とも呼ばれましたが、江戸中期以降「果物」と「菓子」に分化していきました。古くから存在した「くだもの」の語は、その指し示す対象や意味を変えながら生き抜いてきたことばだったと言えるでしょう。

　青森が誇る林檎は『和名抄』に「林檎　リンゴウ」とあります。中国語音ではリンキン、リンゴンと読まれますが後者が転じてリンゴとなったようです。苺は古く『日本書紀』（720年）に「イチビコ」と称されて登場しますが、『本草和名』（901～923年頃）には、現代語同様の「イチゴ」と出てきます。蜜柑は『日葡辞書』（1603年）に「miccan」と記され、室町期にはミッカンと発音したようです。夏の代表的な果物の西瓜は、義堂周信（1325～1388年）が漢詩集『空華集』で「西瓜」を詠んでいますので、南北朝時代には伝来していたようです。身近な「くだもの」の背景も奥深いですね。

24 「呼称」をめぐって
受け継がれる配慮の言語

　「I love you.」。英語では恋人でも夫婦でも親子でも、話者は常にI（私）で相手はyou（あなた）です。仏語でIはJe、中国語で我、と自身を表現します。しかし日本語では、自分の子供相手に話す場合は、「私」を使わずに「ママは」「お父さんは」と自分を称し、学校現場では、生徒に向かって「先生は」と表現することが一般的です。日本語の自称は、英語のようにIで固定されておらず、子供にとっての母親や父親という役割、生徒にとっての先生という立場になり替わった表現が使われます。自分は常に自分のはずで不変なのに他者や周囲に影響を受けて流動しているのですね。

　「私」に代表される自称のバリエーションも豊富で、「わたくし」「僕」「俺」「拙者」、津軽方言の「わ」「おら」など実際の会話では様々なことばが使われています。相手との関係性や距離感によって使い分けているのではないでしょうか。

　日本では夫婦に子供が誕生すると、お互いを「パパ（お父さん）」「ママ（お母さん）」と呼び合う光景も見られます。赤ちゃんからみての祖母はそれまで「お母さん」と呼ばれていたのに自分の子供か

らも「お婆ちゃん」と呼ばれるようになります。赤ちゃんに同調した
呼称に変貌するのです。自己が固定された英語と違い、日本語では他
者から見た自分が優先されます。

　夫が妻を紹介する場合、「家内」「女房」だけでなく、最近は「妻」「嫁
さん」「うちの奥さん」を使う方が増えています。本来、他の人の伴
侶を指す「嫁」「奥さん」を自分の妻に使うのは誤用のはず。敬称「さん」
を付して他人を装うのは妻への配慮でしょうか。あるいは微妙な距離
感でしょうか。「女房」は中世以降に職業名から転用されたことば。「家
内」は明治中期まで「家内安全」と使うように「家庭」を意味しまし
たが、home の訳語に家庭が定着して以降、家内が妻の意を担いまし
た。「ワイフ」を使う知人もいて、妻の呼称も人それぞれ。面白いで
すね。

　日本語は呼称に限らず、会話の相手や場面、心理的距離感を瞬時に
判断し、他者へ配慮した使用を心がけてきた言語だと言えそうです。
普段無意識に使っていることばの不思議。過去を知り、今を再考し、
未来にどうつなげていくか。受け継がれてきた日本語の背景に思いを
馳せ、これからも大切に使ってほしいと願っています。

　ことば探求の旅に一年間おつきあいいただきありがとうございまし
た。

第2章

ことば不思議発見

1 京ことば
方言に自負と卑下

　関西生まれで関西育ちの私が、東北青森の弘前に赴任して講義をはじめた頃のこと。学生たちから「生の関西弁に感激した」と言われました。授業内容より言葉の印象が相当強かったようです。私自身は一生懸命「共通語」で講義していたつもりなのですが…。関西人はいつでもどこでも関西弁のため、厚かましいと誤解されることが多いようです。

　時は鎌倉時代…。日蓮と仙覚という高名な僧侶がいました。出身は共に関東。当時の共通語（中央語）は都のあった京都のことばでしたから、彼らは今でいう方言を話していました。

　日蓮は京都で修行する弟子に向かって諭します。「京都なまりになってはいけません。田舎ことばが良いのです」。京都ことばを「なまる」と評するほど自分のことばに誇りを持っていました。一方の仙覚は劣等感から「関東語の発音が卑しいのは音韻変化の結果」と弁解しています。方言を話す二人が、自負と卑下という正反対の気持ちを持っていたのです。

　さて関西人の私には、日蓮のような自尊心だけでも、仙覚のような卑下心だけでもなく、両方が混在しているようです。青森に来て初めて見直した自分のことば。方言と共通語、皆さんは意識したことがありますか？

2 日本語
単一言語は珍しい

　「あなたは何語を話しますか？」…。ほとんどの人が日本語を使う日本では愚問ですが、フランス語、オランダ語の両方が話されるベルギーでは国勢調査の質問項目になっています。東部の国境付近にはドイツ語を話す地域まであります。

　世界には3000〜6000の言語があると言われていますが、そのような中で日本のような例は少数派なのです。

　スイスの友人宅へ行くことになった時のことです。中国では中国語を、スペインではスペイン語が話されると単純に考えていた父に「スイスはスイス語か？」と真顔で尋ねられました。

　実はスイス語と呼ばれることばはなく、幾つかの言語が使われています。多くの国際機関があるジュネーブではフランス語です。加えて国民の約7割近くがドイツ語を、約1割がイタリア語を話します。国語とされている言語は、これらに古代ラテン語の名残があるロマンシュ語を加えると4つもあります。

　欧州は、隣国と地続きの国がほとんど。2か国語以上を併記した道路標識もよく見かけます。このように国内にことばの壁があると現実の生活では苦労しそうです。日本では日本語さえ話せれば、英語が苦手でも平気。良かったですね。

3 仮名
時間と労力を節約

　昔、漢字は「真実の文字」という意味で「真名（まな）」と呼ばれ、ひらがなやカタカナは「仮の文字」という意味で「仮名（かな）」と呼ばれました。

　画数の多い漢字は、筆で小さく書くのに苦労します。そんなとき、補助的に使えるようにと工夫したのが、仮名の始まりです。

　ひらがなは、草書体という崩し書きの漢字を基にして作られた文字です。例えば「あ」は「安」、「い」は「以」、「う」は「宇」の崩し字が次第に変化してきたものです。一方、カタカナは、漢字のへんなど一部分を省略したもので、「ア」は「阿」の「こざとへん」、「イ」は「伊」の「にんべん」、「ウ」は「うかんむり」が基になっています。これらは、時間と労力を節約する大変合理的な発想で、不便を解消する偉大な創造でした。

　最古の仮名交じり文は、法話の草稿資料『東大寺諷誦文稿』で平安時代初期に書かれました。その後、僧侶たちの間から次第に広まっていきました。

　カタカナは、実用性から仏教の世界や貴族社会で重宝されました。ひらがなは、曲線の多い柔らかな字体が女性に好まれ、日記や和歌を通して日常生活に取り入れられました。現在、使い分けられる仮名2種はこうした古い歴史を背負っているのです。

漢字
意味表し誤解防ぐ

「かれはかいしゃにはいらない」。この文をどう解釈しますか？　「会社に入らない」と読んだ人は「特定の会社を選ばず、自らの意思でやるべき仕事を決めた」と思うでしょう。しかし「会社には要らない」と読めば「リストラされる会社員」が連想されます。このように、誤解を受けないような文章にするためには、漢字が重要な役割を果たしていることがわかるでしょう。

　漢字は、発音と意味を同時に表す表意（表語）文字に当たります。世界のほとんどの文字は、アルファベットのように発音だけを表す表音文字で、ひらがなやカタカナもこちらに属します。日本語のように違う種類の文字を混用するのはほかに例がありません。

　それは、固有の文字がなかったことが原因と言えるでしょう。初めは中国の漢字から音や意味を借用しました。それが、発音だけを表し、簡単に書けるように改良されたのが仮名です。生まれと育ちの違う文字が、長い年月を経て融合され、交ぜ書き表記になりました。

　明治時代には、欧米化を求める風潮の中で、英語の国語化が提案されたり、漢字排斥運動も起こったりしました。このようなことが実現しなかったことにほっとしている私です。

5 なまめかしい
「清純な美」が変化

　平安時代に書かれた『伊勢物語』に、「なまめいた女」に一目ぼれした男が熱烈な恋文をおくる話があります。学生たちにその女性像を想像してもらったところ、叶姉妹や川島なお美、藤原紀香という名前が挙がりました。彼らは、「艶めかしい女」、年上の官能的な女性を思い浮かべたようです。

　『今昔物語』では「生メカシ」と一部に漢字が当てられています。実は、「なまめく女」の「なま」は「生」に通じ、自然そのままの姿を指すのです。成熟した色っぽさとは対極の、若々しい清純な女性が「なまめく女」の正体です。

　日本語を学ぶためイエズス会の宣教師が1603年に作った『日葡辞書』では、「ナマメカシイ」を「愛敬があって美しいこと」と説明しています。この時代でも「色っぽい、妖艶な」という美意識に限定されてはいませんでした。

　「なまめく」は、今も昔も「美しい」という意味に違いはありません。しかし、若い清純な美しさから成熟した美しさへと、本質的な意味内容や印象が大きく変化してしまったのです。

　さて、そうなると冒頭で述べた『伊勢物語』に出てくる女性は、学生たちの予想した姿とは大きく違っていたことになりますね。

6 孤立語
先祖不明の日本語

「目はお父さん、口元はお母さん、性格は誰に似たのかしら!?」。今のあなたは両親から遺伝した部分と生まれてから獲得した個性が共存しています。実は言語も、特徴を分析すると先祖や親類のように分類できます。

これが比較言語学という研究で、言語を家族ならぬ「語族」で種別します。英語やフランス語、ドイツ語などは親戚同士でインド・ヨーロッパ語族に属します。

しかし、日本語は未だに親兄弟がはっきりしていません。そのような言語は寂しく孤独なので「孤立語」とも呼ばれます。「日本語は難しい」と言われますが、似た言語がないことが一因でしょう。

同じ島国でありながら英語は海外への普及が目覚ましく、国外でほとんど使用されない日本語とは対照的です。

世界共通語といわれる英語ですが、話す人が最も多いのは中国語です。英語は2番目。以下スペイン語、ヒンディー語、ロシア語と続き、日本語は9番目。ドイツ語やフランス語よりも話す人が多いのです。

大きな経済成長を遂げたことで、日本語は注目される言語の一つになっています。普段何気なく使っている日本語が、世界でどう位置づけられるのか、考えてみるのも面白いのではないでしょうか。

7 たたみ
フランス語に定着

　古くから日本の生活に欠かせない床材の「畳」。「たたむ」という動詞が名詞化したことばです。今と違って畳は「たためる」敷物のたぐいを指していました。

　平安時代、貴族の住居だった寝殿造りの内部はすべて板の間。必要に応じて畳が敷かれたり、置かれたりしました。昔、畳は座具であり寝具でもあったのです。畳が敷き詰められるようになったのは、書院造りが完成した鎌倉時代から室町時代にかけてです。そして現代のように一般庶民の生活にも身近になったのは、江戸時代中期以降でした。

　実は「tatami」は、海外で日本文化を表すキーワードになっています。フランス語の新造語「tatamiser」は、日本風の生活様式や室内装飾を取り入れることを指します。これは逆輸入され、現代用語を解説する事典などには外来語「タタミゼ」として掲載されています。

　このように日本文化普及の一翼を担う畳ですが、本家の日本では最近、出番が少なくなりました。ある時は座卓を置いて食事室に、ある時は一家団欒の居間に、そして布団を敷くと寝室に早変わり。日本の狭い住空間を上手く利用する、日本の生活様式に合った畳。大いに誇るべき文化の一つではないでしょうか。

着物と服
流行で意味も変化

　日本の衣裳「着物」は、英語でもそのまま「kimono（きもの）」として受け入れられています。このことばが現在のように和服を指すようになったのは、明治時代に受けた西洋文明の影響が大きいのです。

　江戸時代のことばの教養書『かたこと』には「家の衣類をきものといふ」とあります。「着物」は本来、衣服すべてを指すことばだったのです。幕末に来日した宣教師のヘボンの作った辞書『和英語林集成』は、1867年の初版には「きもの」「服」が載っていましたが、19年後に出された第3版には「洋服」も登場。この間に欧風の生活スタイルが定着した様子がうかがえます。

　服と着物は、両方とも衣類の総称でした。しかし、日常生活で洋服を着る方が多くなるに従い、服は洋服だけを指すようになります。二葉亭四迷の小説『浮雲』には「男は和服に着替え、脱ぎ捨てた服をたたみ」との文が見られます。一方、着物は次第に和服に限って使われるようになり、服と着物の関係は変化していきました。

　流行を表す「モード」が、特に服装のことを指すように、衣類に関することばは社会情勢に左右されやすいようです。裏返せば、適応力に富み、時代をすぐに反映するとも言えるのです。

9 ふとん
座具の意から変化

　日本人にとって、誰もが身近な寝具の「蒲団」。「蒲」は植物のガマで「団」は団子から連想されるように「丸い」という意味。だから昔の蒲団は丸かったはず…、です。

　鎌倉時代、禅宗とともに日本に入ってきた蒲団は、唐宋音で「ふとん」と読まれました。禅宗の一派である曹洞宗の開祖、道元の書いた『正法眼蔵』には「座禅のとき、袈裟をかくべし、蒲団をしくべし」とあります。蒲団は、座禅のときにお尻にあてがう、ガマで編んだ丸い敷物のことだったのです。その後、語形を変えることなく、指し示すものが座具から寝具へ変化していきました。

　寝具に変わってきたのは、江戸時代。蒲団は、遊女たちの人気を測るバロメーターにもなっていました。彼女たちは、客にねだって蒲団をプレゼントされていたのです。江戸川柳「三つ蒲団　うんと言ったがそれっきり」と一番人気を争う彼女たちと、ごひいきの客との駆け引きの様子を皮肉ったものがあります。

　意味が寝具に代わったことで素材が変わり、ガマとは無関係になります。このため「蒲で編まれた敷物」という原義は忘れ去られ、新たに「布団」という漢字表記が生まれたのです。

10 だんな
「尊敬表現」今は昔

　「女房と畳は新しい方がいい、なんて言うけれど、最近はだんなとキッチンは新しい方がいいんですってよ〜」。個性派女優の市原悦子さんが叫ぶテレビＣＭがありました。妻の発言権が大きくなった家族関係を示していて、笑わせますね。

　「だんな」は、仏教とともに輸入された梵語（サンスクリット）から来たことばです。「与える」という意味の「dana」に漢字が当てられました。平安時代は、お寺に贈る布施や檀家を意味し、「檀那」という漢字が使われました。それが次第に「後援者」「雇い主」と意味を広げ、目上の人を指す尊敬表現として日常語になっていき、「旦那」も使われるようになります。

　現代語のように「夫」を指す呼称として使われ始めたのは、江戸時代中期のことでした。それからは時代を経るにつれて、よく使われるようになり、ことばに含まれる敬意の度合いが低くなっていきました。最近は女性の社会的地位が向上した世相を反映し、妻の側からの親しみを込めた表現としての「だんな」も存在しているようです。

　冒頭のＣＭでは、改まった会話でも使える「主人」や「夫」では、雰囲気が台無し。ことばの選択は、印象が違うだけでなく、話し手の意識も表しているのですね。

11 おにぎり
関西発信の呼び名

　コンビニの売れ筋商品の一つ「おにぎり」。今やおふくろの味も街の至るところで売られる時代になったようです。

　この便利な携帯食は昔、「にぎりいひ(握り飯)」と呼ばれていました。手に取ると飯粒がくっつくところから、奈良時代頃に書かれた『常陸風土記』には「にぎりいひ　筑波の国といふ」と、筑波の枕詞的に使われた例が見られます。

　「いひ（飯）」と呼ばれたご飯は「こはいひ（強飯）」、さらに鎌倉室町時代になると「めし（飯）」と変化しました。「おにぎり」も「にぎりいひ」から「にぎりめし」を経て、短縮形の「にぎり」に丁寧の接頭語「お」を付けて「おにぎり」となったのです。

　「おむすび」も、平安時代の女性たちが使っていた古いことばです。しかし「おにぎり」という呼び方が関西に登場すると、「おむすび」を抑えて勢力を拡大し、全国に広まったようです。ただ地域によって「にぎりめし」のほか「にぎりまんま」「にんに」などという呼び方が残っています。

　アメリカでは「rice ball（ライスボール）」と呼ばれています。便利な日本の携行食は、海外でも、もっと普及するかもしれませんね。

12 女房詞
にょうぼうことば
宮中の「業界用語」

　『源氏物語』を書いた紫式部や『枕草子』の作者清少納言は、平安時代に活躍した女性です。彼女たちは、天皇や上皇の御所に仕える位の高い女官で「女房」と呼ばれました。

　女房たちは、水のことを「おひや」、腹を「おなか」と言い換えるなど、自分たちだけで通じる生活用語を使っていました。このようなことばを「女房詞」と総称します。もともと仲間内で使った隠語のたぐいであり、いわば「業界用語」だったのです。

　例えば、副菜のことを指す「おかず」もその一つです。当時の食事は、いくつもの小皿に分けて、配膳台の上に乗せられていました。「おかず」は、「配膳台の上にある数々のもの」という意味で、「かず」に丁寧表現の接頭語「お」が付けられて作られました。

　このように女房たちは、直接的な表現を避け、婉曲的な言い方を次々に考え出しました。それが次第に公家や武家、そして庶民にまで女性の使う上品な表現として広がっていったのです。

　それから千年以上を経て、生活様式が全く変わってしまった現代。今なお、宮中の女性たちが生み出したことばが、社会に溶け込んでいるのは大変な驚きですね。

13 美人
若い男性も対象に

「美人」と言われて悪い気のする女性はいるでしょうか。これは、容姿端麗な女性を指すことばですが、美しい「人」ですから、本来は男女どちらでもいいはずです。

「美」にはそれだけでなく、「うまい、大きい、立派な」という意味もあります。中国の古典で、才徳を備えた賢人も「美人」と呼ばれていることにも通じています。

日本では、女性のことに使われるように思われていますが、室町から江戸時代にかけて、独特の用法が見られます。室町時代に禅僧たちが作った、中国の書物の注釈資料『詩学大成抄』には「美人は美しい女性のこと。日本のように、稚児若衆を美人とは言わないぞ」というくだりがあります。当時は、少年に対しても「美人」を使っていたようです。

江戸時代の例では、仮名草子『心友記』に「ひとり息子の重光殿は、十四歳で美人である」とあります。また元禄期に浮世草子を書いた井原西鶴も「美人のご子息」「その美人のご二男の名は？」など、男性を表現していました。「美人」は、若い男性も対象にしていたようです。

現代は、女性を指す場合がほとんど。しかし、表面的な美しさだけでなく、本来の意味の才能や人徳も備えた本当の美人でありたいですね。

14 恋
孤独の切なさ表現

　「恋は盲目」は、恋が理性や分別を失わせることを意味する英国のことわざです。日本では浄瑠璃に「恋の一念」ということばが使われており、恋の情熱的な一面を表しています。

　しかし、もともと「恋」は「静かな悲しみ」という心情に比重が置かれていました。『万葉集』には、「孤悲（こひ）」という表記が見られます。当時の人たちがこのことばに込めた思いをよく表したものと言えるでしょう。これは「孤独を悲しむ気持ち、恋しい相手が目の前にいないことを寂しく思い、求め慕う」という心情です。

　異性に限らず、自然や風物も恋の対象になりました。心惹かれる人や物と一緒にいたいという願いを果たせず、心に生じた孤独で切ない気持ち。これが「恋」の核心だったのです。

　江戸時代後期の国学者、本居宣長でさえ、「人の情の感ずる事、恋に勝るはなし」と言っています。恋は人の感情を豊かにするので存在意義は非常に大きいと説いているのです。

　「孤悲」に秘められた、昔の人の思い。宣長も「人生に必要不可欠」と応援しています。ただ、日本の伝統的な恋は、理性や分別を失わず、悲哀を受け止め、自分の心を見つめる精神性が大切だったようです。

15 えりすぐり
母音が次第に変化

　特に良い物を選び出すことを「えりすぐり」または「よりすぐり」
と言います。国語辞典には、意味の違いは載っていません。あなたは、
どちらを使っていますか？

　平安時代末期の歴史書『栄華物語』に「えりすぐりてしらせ給ひ」
とあるように、古語では「選る（える）」の複合語でした。これに対
して「よる」には選ぶという意味はなく、「えりすぐり」が原形だっ
たのです。

　室町時代の日本語をポルトガル語で解説した辞書には「yerivzqe
（えりわけ）」という語が載っています。当時は「えり分ける」の「え」
は「ye（イェ）」という発音に近かったようです。これが次第に「yo」
に変化し、「よ」になりました。

　「選ぶ」という意味の「よる」は、こうして誕生したのです。この
ような変化は母音交替と呼ばれ、室町時代のことばによく見られます。

　江戸時代に流行した説経浄瑠璃『小栗判官』などでは、「よりすぐり」
が使われています。このころには両方とも使われていたのでしょう。

　ことばは移り変わるもの。どちらが正しいと厳格に規定できない場
合もあります。ただ、今回のことで私は意識して原形の「えりすぐり」
を使うようになりました。

16 花笑う
「咲」が「笑」の基に

　漢字は一般に、へんが意味を表し、つくりが音を表すと言われます。「花が咲く」と書くときの「咲」には、口へんが使われていますが、口に関係する意味があるとは思えませんね。実は、「咲」は「笑」の基になった本字。昔、口に関連する「わらう」という意味があったのです。

　平安時代の辞書『観智院本類聚名義抄』には「咲」に「わらふ、えむ」などと注釈されています。確かに同じ頃の説話『今昔物語集』では「わらう」に「咲ふ」が使われています。

　花が開く意味の「咲く」という使い方が定着したのは、江戸時代のようです。このころに作られた辞書『書言字考節用集』には「咲く」に「さく」と読みが振られています。

　寡黙を好む日本人には「わらう」という意味の漢字は「笑」で十分だったからでしょうか。あるいは花が「うふふ」とほほ笑んだように感じて、誰かが使い始めたのかもしれません。

　「咲」のように、本家中国とは違う意味で使われている漢字を国訓、または借訓と言います。「鮎」は日本では「アユ」ですが、中国では「ナマズ」。意外ですね。

17 青
意味する幅が縮小

　憂うつな気分を「ブルーな気分」と表現することがあります。流行語などを解説した事典によると、色彩だけを表していた「ブルー」が近年は心情にも使われるようになったことが記されています。色を示すことばが心情まで表すように、意味や用法が拡大した一例です。

　一方、意味の幅が縮小した例が「ブルー」の翻訳語「青」で見られます。日本語では、青はとても重要なことばでした。古代には、現在「緑」や「灰色」と呼ばれる色を含めた幅広い色を「青」が表していたのです。もともと、色として独立した名前があったのは「赤」「黒」「白」「青」の４種だけ。ほかの多くの色は、これらで表現していました。

　『万葉集』に「緑子（みどりご）」ということばが見られます。「若々しい新芽のような未熟な子ども」という意味です。この用法が次第に「緑」単独で、若葉の色を指すことばとなったようです。平安時代以降に作られた勅撰和歌集では、「青」の頻度が減り、代わりに「緑」が登場します。もともと「青」に含まれていた色が、独立していったのです。

　現在でも、信号機の緑色を「青」と呼ぶように、厳格に区別しない用法があります。これは、昔の色彩語の名残なのかもしれませんね。

18 風呂敷
江戸期の敷物由来

　私が結婚するとき、家紋や名前を染め抜いた風呂敷や贈り物などを包む袱紗を作って持たされました。「今どき使うことあるのかしら」と思いましたが、親を不機嫌にさせたくはなかったので、素直に従いました。

　風呂敷は、正方形の布地です。一般に広まったのは、江戸時代半ばの元禄期。現在は和服を着るようなときに使われることが多いのですが、当時はより生活に密着した存在でした。

　初めは、銭湯の脱衣所で敷物として使われました。脱いだ衣類を包み、湯上りにはタオル代わりにも使ったようです。「風呂」で「敷く」から、「風呂敷」だったのですね。江戸時代後期の辞書『書言字考節用集』には、「風呂敷」が登場しています。

　さて、この風呂敷、どんな形の物でも包むことができ、使い終わると小さくたたむことができます。しかも何度も使えます。要らなくなったら、捨ててしまう紙袋やレジ袋よりも、環境には随分、優しいですね。

　せっかく作ってもらった我が家の風呂敷ですが、タンスにしまったまま、ほとんど出番がありません。ただ、資源を無駄にしないためにも、親心が込められたこの風呂敷をもっと使ってみようかと、あらためて考えています。

19 辞書
「右」の表現も多彩

　教育学部の教員だった私が、附属小学校で研究授業をしたときのこと。それまで小中学校や高校で教壇に立ったことがなかったのでとても緊張しました。それでも、ことばに対する子どもたちへの探求心を養うのに少しは役に立てたと思います。

　授業のテーマは「辞書であそぼう」。わからないことばをただ引くのではなく、説明を「読む」授業です。どの辞書も、書かれている意味は同じと思われがちですが、比べてみると意外に興味深い読み物であることがわかります。

　例えば「右」ということばを調べてみましょう。ある辞書では「大部分の人が、はしやペンを持つ方」「北を向いたとき、東にあたる方」などと出ています。

　別の辞書では「南向きに立つとき、西にあたる方」「日本の道路で、車が走るのと逆側」と説明。さらに「この辞書を開いて読む時、奇数ページのある方」「アナログ時計の文字盤に向ったときに、一時から五時までの表示のある側」なども…。

　それぞれに工夫があり、個性ある説明が見られますね。誰もが理解している「右」ということばですが、うまく説明するのは案外難しそうです。皆さんなら、どう表現しますか？

20 便所
負の印象　敬遠続く

　築40年以上経った弘前大学教育学部の校舎。和式トイレの扉には「便所」の文字。弘前大学理工学部の校舎のトイレは温水洗浄装置付きの新型で、扉の表示は文字でなく絵（サイン）です。直接的な表現のためか、最近「便所」のことばは敬遠されているようです。

　トイレは昔、「厠（かわや）」と呼ばれました。室町時代の辞書『下学集（かがくしゅう）』には、「河屋（かわや）」とあります。小川をまたいで用をたしている人の脚の形を建物の屋根に例えたのが語源のようです。禅宗の寺院では、僧侶が修行する伽藍（がらん）の東にあるものを「東司（とうす）」、西なら「西浄（せいじょう）」、北では「雪隠（せっちん）」と呼び分けました。

　戦国時代の軍学書『甲陽軍鑑（こうようぐんかん）』では、武田信玄の使った6畳もある広い便所を「御閑所（ごかんじょ）」と紹介し、直接的な表現が避けられています。「便所」は江戸期以降に普及しますが、それ以前は、これらのように婉曲的な表現が使われていたのです。

　今では「トイレ」という外来語が定着していますが、イメージ向上のため、常に新しい呼び名が求められているようです。本来の目的から離れていますが「化粧室」もそんなことばです。

　たかがトイレ。しかし表示の違いで印象まで変わるのは、ことばのもつ力のせいでしょうか。

（注）2023年現在、弘前大学教育学部校舎は改修され、「便所」の表示はなくなった。

21 鳴き声
擬声表現に地域差

　日本では、犬の鳴き声は「ワンワン」。でも英語では「bowwow(バウワウ)」です。鳴き声が、日本と英、米両国とで違うはずはないのですが、人間がことばで表現すると、全く別になってしまうのは面白い現象ですね。

　ところで、スズメの鳴き声を「チュンチュン」と思っている人は多いでしょう。しかし、鎌倉時代の辞書『名語記（みょうごき）』には、「すずめのなく、しうしう」と記されています。江戸時代の俳諧書『風俗文選（ふうぞくもんぜん）』には、「からすのかあかあと鳴きくらし、すずめのちいちいと同じ事さへづる」と、また別の表現になっています。

　大正時代に作られた唱歌「すずめの学校」では、「ちいちいぱっぱ、ちいぱっぱ、すずめの学校の先生は、むちをふりふりちいぱっぱ」ですね。

　国立国語研究所が1955年ごろに行った方言調査では、関東、中部、四国、九州では「チューチュー」が使われており、「チュンチュン」と表現するのは近畿を中心とした地域だけでした。この近畿流がほかの地域にも広がったのは、ネズミの鳴き声と同じ音になるのを避けた結果なのかもしれません。

　何気なく使っている擬声語ですが、定着するまでにはこうした長い道のりがあったのですね。

22 語彙
日本語がダントツ

フランス語や英語は、1000語覚えれば日常会話の約8割を、5000語で9割以上を理解できると言われます。これに対して、日本語は1000語覚えてもわかるのは6割。9割以上を理解するには、なんと22000語が必要です。いかに日本語の語彙が多いかがわかります。

語彙の多さは、日本語が新しいことばを作りやすい構造であることが理由のひとつです。言い換えれば、日本人はことばを変形させるなどの工夫をすることが上手なのではないでしょうか。

近年、日本語の乱れとして、ことばの誤用が問題視されることが多くなっています。しかし、そもそもことばは変化していくものです。特に日本語は、外国文化を取り入れてことばを増やしてきた歴史があります。

例えば、「愚痴る」は、漢語「愚痴」に日本語の動詞「する」を合成した造語ですが、「文句を言う」という意味で定着しています。今では当たり前のように使われている「メモる」や「サボる」といったことばも、英語やフランス語を変化させた学生ことばから広まりました。

また、サラリーマンやコストダウンなどの和製英語も多数あります。これを日本人の言語意識の低さと見るか、工夫と見るか、は考え方が分かれるかもしれませんね。

23 こわい
「信念強い」の意も

　有名なかぐや姫の物語。彼女のうわさを聞いた天皇が、求愛の使者を差し向けますが、どうしても申し出に応じません。育ての親、竹取の翁は、そんなかぐや姫を「こわい娘だから…。」と弁解するのです。でも、かぐや姫ってそんなに恐ろしかったのでしょうか。

　現在の「こわい」は、「恐ろしい」とほぼ同じ意味で恐怖感を表します。しかし、古語「こはし」は、最古の漢字事典『新撰字鏡』では「堅」「固」とあり、『色葉字類抄』では「強」という漢字が当てられています。基は「堅い」「強い」という、ものの性質や状態を表す形容詞だったのです。

　世界最古の短編小説集といわれる『堤中納言物語』にある「虫愛づる姫君」というお話にも「こわい紙」が出てきます。これは、堅くゴワゴワした紙という意味。かぐや姫の場合も、彼女の性格を表したもので「強情な」と解釈できます。かぐや姫が恐ろしい女性だったのではなく、信念をもっていたことを表現していたのです。

　堅固で強いものに対峙したとき、人は手ごわい相手を恐れる感情が芽生えます。このため、「こわい」ということばは、室町時代以降に「恐ろしい」という心情を表す意味でも使われるようになったようです。

24 カステラ
もともとは外来語

　日本人にはなじみの深いお菓子「カステラ」。外見も名前も洋菓子のようですが、売られているのはもっぱら和菓子屋さん。なぜでしょうか。

　その作り方は、ポルトガル人が江戸時代初めに伝えました。それを「pao de Castella(カスティーリャ王国のパン)」と呼んだのが始まりです。当時の百科事典『和漢三才図会』には「加須底羅」とあり、「カステイラ」と呼ばれました。

　また、茶会の記録『槐記』に「菓子かすてら蒸返し」とあるように茶の湯でも用いられたようです。さらに、江戸時代前期に書かれた『太閤記』には「下戸には、かすていら、ぼうる、こんぺい糖などをもてなし」と一般に広まっている様子が描かれています。

　長崎から、京都、大坂へ…。そして全国各地に広がるうちに、日本人の嗜好に合わせた味に改良されていきました。今では日本独特の菓子のようになっています。和菓子屋で売られているのはこのためですね。

　ほかにも、漢字の表記があるためか、すっかり日本語になじんでしまったポルトガル語起源のことばもあります。「煙草(たばこ)」や「天婦羅(てんぷら)」も、実はそんな外来語なのです。

25 はやて
悪いイメージ脱皮

　東北新幹線が青森八戸まで延びて、もう何年もたちました。首都圏と北東北を結んで疾走する列車には「はやて」という愛称がつけられました。この「はやて」という語は平安時代からある古いことばです。

　もとは「はやち」という「恐ろしい暴れ狂う風」を意味しました。当時の辞書『色葉字類抄』に「暴風」という漢字に「ハヤチ」の読みがあります。また、清少納言の『枕草子』にも「恐ろしきもの」という段に「はやち」が登場するなど、好意的には受け止められていませんでした。

　その後、音韻が変化した「はやて」が定着します。室町時代の辞書『温故知新書』には「疾風」、江戸時代の俳諧書『毛吹草』では「早手」と書かれ、早いことが協調されていった様子が知られます。「暴風」から「疾風」「早手」と変化し、次第に悪いイメージから脱皮していったようです。これからは、新幹線の愛称として駆け抜ける風のような、さわやかなイメージが定着するのではないでしょうか。

　「はやて」は、時代や社会の影響を受けてきました。ことばは使う人の思想や意識に大きく影響されるもの。過去から、現在、未来へと人を通じてつながっていく生きものなのです。

　(注) 2023 年現在、東北新幹線は北海道新函館北斗まで延伸し、「はやて」の愛称は「はやぶさ」へ変更されている。

【 文献一覧 】（掲載順）

- 周易抄　鈴木博『周易抄の国語学的研究　影印篇』清文堂（1972年）
- 日葡辞書　『日葡辞書』勉誠社（1973年）、土井忠生・森田武・長南実編訳『邦訳日葡辞書』岩波書店（1980年）
- 万葉集　『万葉集　訳文・本文篇・各句索引』塙書房（1963年）、新編日本古典文学全集『万葉集1〜4』小学館（1994年）、新日本古典文学大系『万葉集1〜4』岩波書店（2004年）
- 日本霊異記　新編日本古典文学全集『日本霊異記』小学館（1995年）、新日本古典文学大系『日本霊異記』岩波書店（1996年）
- 砂の器　松本清張『砂の器』新潮文庫（1973年）
- 人間の証明　森村誠一『人間の証明』角川文庫（2015年）
- 祖国とは国語　藤原正彦『祖国とは国語』新潮文庫（2005年）
- 哲学字彙　井上哲次郎編『哲学字彙』東京大学（1881年）、『改訂増補哲学字彙』東洋館（1884年）
- 東大寺諷誦文稿　中田祝夫『東大寺諷誦文稿の国語学的研究』風間書房（1969年）
- 源氏物語　新編日本古典文学全集『源氏物語1〜6』小学館（1994年）、新日本古典文学大系『源氏物語1〜5』岩波書店（2017年）
- 今昔物語集　新日本古典文学大系『今昔物語集1〜5』岩波書店（1993年）、新編古典文学全集『今昔物語1〜4』小学館（1999年）
- 平家物語　新日本古典文学大系『平家物語上下』岩波書店（1991年）、新編古典文学全集『平家物語1〜2』小学館（1994年）
- 続日本紀　新日本古典文学大系『続日本紀1〜5』岩波書店（1989年）
- 倭名類聚抄　京都大学文学部国語学国文学研究室編『諸本集成倭名類聚抄　本文篇索引篇』（1968年）、馬淵和夫著『和名類聚抄　声点本本文および索引』風間書房（1973年）馬淵和夫編著『古写本和名類聚抄集成』勉誠出版（2008年）
- 古今著聞集　日本古典文学大系『古今著聞集』岩波書店（1966年）、新潮日本古典集成『古今著聞集　上下』新潮社（1983年）
- 宇治拾遺物語　新日本古典文学大系『宇治拾遺物語・古本説話集』岩波書店（1990年）、新編日本古典文学全集『宇治拾遺物語』小学館（1996年）
- 蕎麦全書　新島繁編『蕎麦うどん名著選集』所収、東京書房社（1981年）、新島繁著『現代語訳蕎麦全書伝』ハート出版（2006年）
- 守貞漫稿　喜田川守貞『近世風俗志1』所収、岩波文庫（1996年）
- 大阪の宿　水上滝太郎『大阪の宿』新潮文庫（1949年）

- 色葉字類抄　中田祝夫・峯岸明編『色葉字類抄　研究並びに索引』風間書房（1964年）
- 易林本節用集　中田祝夫『改訂新版古本節用集　六種　研究並びに総合索引　影印篇』勉誠社（1979年）
- 料理物語　塙保己一『続群書類従19下』所収、続群書類従完成会（1969年）
- 日本の食生活全集　『日本の食生活全集１～50』農山漁村文化協会、（1993年）
- 日本言語地図　国立国語研究所編『日本言語地図１～６』大蔵省印刷局（1981年）
- 日本語語感の辞典　中村明著『日本語語感の辞典』岩波書店（2010年）
- 女寺子調法記　『重宝記資料集成８』所収、臨川書店（2005年）
- 和英語林集成　Ｊ・Ｃ・ヘボン『和英語林集成』東洋文庫復刻版（1872年）、『和英語林集成（第３版）』講談社学術文庫（1980年）
- 観智院本類聚名義抄　『類聚名義抄　観智院本』新天理図書館善本叢書（2018年）
- 文明本節用集　中田祝夫著『文明本節用集　研究並びに索引　索引篇・影印篇』風間書房（1970年）
- 書言字考節用集　中田祝夫・小林洋次郎著『書言字考節用集　研究並びに索引　索引篇・影印篇』風間書房（1973年）
- 日本大文典　Ｊ・ロドリゲス原著　土井忠生訳注『日本大文典』三省堂（1955年）
- 枕草子　新日本古典文学大系『枕草子』岩波書店（1991年）、新編日本古典文学全集『枕草子』小学館（1997年）
- 万葉のいぶき　犬養孝『万葉のいぶき』新潮文庫（1983年）
- 古典対照語い表　宮島達夫編『古典対照語い表』笠間書院（1971年）
- 春秋左氏伝　『春秋左氏伝　上中下』岩波文庫（1988年）
- 古事記　日本古典文学大系『古事記　祝詞』岩波書店（1958年）、新編日本古典文学全集『古事記』小学館（1997年）
- 桃花源記　『陶淵明全集　下』所収、岩波文庫（1990年）
- 古今和歌集　新日本古典文学大系『古今和歌集』岩波書店（1989年）、新編日本古典文学全集『古今和歌集』小学館（1994年）
- 農林水産省　作況調査（2021年）「令和２年産果樹生産出荷統計」https://www.e-stat.go.jp/stat-search/files?tclass=000001149421&cycle=7&year=20200（最終閲覧日：2023年12月１日）
- 謡曲『善知鳥』　野上豊一郎編『謡曲全集』所収、中央公論社（1986年）
- 謡曲拾葉集　『日本文学古註釈大成』所収、日本図書センター（1979年）

・運歩色葉集　中田祝夫・根上剛士著『中世古辞書　四種　研究並びに総合索引　索引篇・影印篇』風間書房（1971年）

・日本国語大辞典　『日本国語大辞典（第2版）1～13』小学館（2000～2002年）

・胡瓜遣　『明治の文学1』所収、筑摩書房（1965年）

・鹿角方言考　大里武八郎『鹿角方言考』鹿角方言考刊行会（1953年）

・境港市史　『境港市史　上下』境港市（1986年）

・伊京集　中田祝夫『古本節用集六種研究並びに総合索引　影印篇』風間書房（1968年）

・津軽　『太宰治全集7』所収、筑摩書房（1989年）、『津軽』新潮文庫（1951年）

・走れメロス　『太宰治全集3』所収、筑摩書房（1989年）、『走れメロス』新潮文庫（2005年）

・こころ　『定本漱石全集9』所収、岩波書店（2017年）、『こころ』新潮文庫（2004年）

・舞姫　『森鷗外全集1』所収、筑摩書房（1995年）、『阿部一族・舞姫』新潮文庫（2006年）

・羅生門　『芥川龍之介全集1』岩波書店（1995年）、『羅生門・鼻』新潮文庫（2005年）

・富岳百景　『太宰治全集2』所収、筑摩書房（1989年）、『富岳百景・走れメロス他8篇』岩波文庫（1957年）

・女生徒　『太宰治全集2』所収、筑摩書房（1989年）、『女生徒』角川文庫（2009年）

・葉桜と魔笛　『太宰治全集2』所収、筑摩書房（1989年）

・雀　『太宰治全集8』所収、筑摩書房（1989年）

・トカトントン　『太宰治全集8』所収、筑摩書房（1989年）

・待つ　『太宰治全集5』所収、筑摩書房（1989年）

・水仙　『太宰治全集5』所収、筑摩書房（1989年）

・畜犬談　『太宰治全集3』所収、筑摩書房（1989年）

・荊楚歳時記　守屋美都雄訳注『荊楚歳時記』東洋文庫（1978年）

・和蘭問答　『海表叢書2』所収、更生閣書店（1928年）

・蘭説弁惑　『紅毛雑話・蘭説弁惑』八坂書房（1972年）

・西洋衣食住　『福沢諭吉全集2』所収、岩波書店（1969年）

・字鏡集　中田祝夫・林義雄著『字鏡集白河本寛元本研究並びに総合索引2　影印篇』勉誠社（1978年）

- 蜻蛉日記　新日本古典文学大系『土佐日記　蜻蛉日記　紫式部日記　更級日記』岩波書店（1989年）、新編日本古典文学全集『土佐日記・蜻蛉日記』小学館（1995年）
- 名語記　田山方南校閲・北野克写『名語記』勉誠社（1983年）
- 本草和名　丸山裕美子編著『本草和名　影印・翻刻と研究』汲古書院（2021年）
- 空華集　上村観光編『五山文学全集2版』所収、思文閣（1992年）
- 伊勢物語　新編日本古典文学全集『竹取物語　伊勢物語　大和物語　平中物語』小学館（1994年）、新日本古典文学大系『竹取物語　伊勢物語』岩波書店（1997年）
- かたこと　『覆刻日本古典文学全集　片言　物類称呼　浪速聞書く　丹波通辞附補遺』現代思潮新社（2006年）
- 浮雲　『二葉亭四迷全集1』所収、岩波書店（1964年）
- 正法眼蔵　『正法眼蔵1〜4』岩波文庫（1990年）
- 常陸風土記　『常陸国風土記』山川出版社（2007年）
- 詩学大成抄　柳田征司『詩学大成抄の国語学的研究　影印篇上下』清文堂（1975年）
- 心友記　長友千代治編『心友記・好色破邪顕正』和泉書院（1987年）
- 栄華物語　日本古典文学大系『栄華物語　上下』岩波書店（1964年）、新編日本古典文学全集『栄華物語1〜3』小学館（1998年）
- 下学集　中田祝夫・林義雄著『古本下学集　七種　研究並びに総合索引』風間書房（1971年）
- 甲陽軍鑑　佐藤正英校訂『甲陽軍鑑』ちくま学芸文庫（2006年）
- 風俗文選　『風俗文選』岩波文庫（1928年）
- 新撰字鏡　京都大学文学部国語学国文学研究室編『天治本　新撰字鏡　増訂版』臨川書店（1975年）
- 堤中納言物語　新日本古典文学体系『堤中納言物語　とりかへばや物語』岩波書店（1992年）、新編日本古典文学全集『落窪物語　堤中納言物語』小学館（2000年）
- 和漢三才図会　東洋文庫『和漢三才図会』平凡社（1985年）
- 槐記　日本古典文学大系『近世随想集』所収、岩波書店（1965年）
- 太閤記　小瀬甫庵原著・吉田豊訳『太閤記』教育社新書（1979年）
- 温故知新書　中田祝夫・根上剛士著『中世古辞書　四種　研究並びに総合索引　索引篇・影印篇』風間書房（1971年）
- 毛吹草　『毛吹草』岩波文庫（1943年）

Professor Kohri's Travels
A Quest for Words

We are くだもの

Authors

·

Kohri Chizuko
Tada Megumi
Berman, Shari Joy

Professor Kohri's Travels: A Quest for Words 〈Contents〉

Contents

Introduction

Having a language is an innate characteristic of human beings. Language is an indispensable means of communication. However, most of us probably use it in many different ways without even thinking about it.

Innovations in science and technology are advancing at a tremendous pace. Just look at the development of the internet, AI, robots, space rockets, etc. Research in the medical and pharmaceutical fields has also made dramatic strides, with a plethora of new treatment methods. On the other hand, how much do we understand about something as simple as our mother tongue, Japanese? We use it every day, do we not? Surprisingly, there are many things we do not know. Researchers in the field of Japanese linguistics, including myself, are constantly trying to solve the mysteries of the meaning behind those words we take for granted.

In recent years, academic research that is immediately useful to society tends to be everyone's main focus. The significance of research fields such as literature, language, and art, the usefulness of which is difficult to see, is frequently questioned. However, I believe that the one issue that has remained unchanged since the birth of humankind is the need to learn how to live well. We are born, we are loved, we love, we mature while rejoicing, grieving, and worrying; then we grow old and die. Whether we live in country with all the modern conveniences or in the more remote areas of the earth, the act of living as a human being is the same and has been in every age. Most of us believe that literature and art can enrich people's sensibilities, nurture their imagination and creativity, and influence them to lead a good life.

Have you ever had the experience of being listened to and encouraged by someone when you were mentally or physically exhausted? Did you wonder how they found the energy to be so kind and understanding? To look at this another way, have you ever been hurt by a thoughtless word? Words have power. They can encourage people, but they can also bring them down. The purpose of this work is to empower you. We hope that you will learn a few things about the essence of the Japanese language, the words that you use every day. We hope that these little history lessons will help you feel both the effects and the charm of the Japanese language.

Learning about the Japanese language also should lead you to thinking about Japan and the Japanese people. The second half of the book is in English, as we hope that international students studying Japanese, or about Japan, as well as those overseas who are interested in Japan will have the opportunity to read this. I would like to thank Professor Megumi Tada and Rabbi (Professor) Shari Joy Berman, who created the English version. While discussing the translation, we have tried to make the English version easier to understand and read for non-native Japanese readers. The English version is also annotated to enable readers to learn about classical Japanese literature and history as well as to understand more about the Japanese language.

This is a journey of exploration through words that you can embark upon in both Japanese and English. We hope that readers will discover that the seeds of curiosity are hidden even in familiar words and experience the joy of imagining and thinking together. We hope to show you that each common word discussed has its own mysterious and colorful story, and that the heart of the user is expressed in the words.

The first part of this book is a collection of essays entitled "Professor Kohri's Travels: a Quest for Words," which appeared in the cultural section of the Toō Nippō Newspaper (Aomori) for one year between September 2021 and August 2022. The main title for these essays with my name on them was created by the newspaper, but I have also used the topic names and the subtitles of each essay as was produced by the editor. The cute illustrations were provided by Makiko Tsuchiya, a graduate student at Hirosaki University at the time. Part 2, "Discovering the Wonder of Language," was a series of articles I wrote as associate professor at the request of the Culture Department of Jiji Press (Tokyo). They asked me to write a column explaining words in a way that junior high school students could understand. These short columns were then distributed to local newspapers throughout Japan. The first series of essays were written with a regional flavor, with readers living in Aomori Prefecture in mind. The second part was written with a singular focus due to the limited number of words. Ms. Tsuchiya drew new illustrations for the book since the person in charge of illustrations at the time could not be reached. Due to the nature of a newspaper series, current events of the time influenced what was covered, so there are some inconsistencies between what appeared in the original and the current version. However, please understand that we have attempted to respect the original text.

Finally, I would like to take this opportunity to thank Toō Nippō Newspaper and Jiji Press for their kind permission to republish these serialized manuscripts. Furthermore, I would like to thank Hirosaki University Press editor-in-chief, Professor Akiko Kashiwagi, Professor Mitsuteru Sato, Professor Sōsuke Iwai, and all of the faculty members who were very helpful in the publication process. In writing this manuscript, I also refer frequently to the accumulated research of our predecessors. Unfortunately, it is not possible to mention everyone by name. Finally, I would like to express my sincere gratitude to the many people whose help and support has made this publication possible.

Completed in the beautiful Hirosaki autumn, 2023.

Kohri Chizuko

History of Japan

Paleothic period	石器時代	circa B.C. 14,000
Jomon period	縄文時代	circa B.C. 14,000 - 10th century B.C.
Yayoi period	弥生時代	circa 10th century B.C. - 3rd century B.C.
Tumulus period	古墳時代	circa mid-3rd century - 7th century
Asuka period	飛鳥時代	592-710
Nara period	奈良時代	710-794
Heian period	平安時代	794-1185
Kamakura period	鎌倉時代	1185-1333
Kenmu New Government	建武の新政	1333-1336
Nanbokuchō period	南北朝時代	1336-1392
Muromachi period	室町時代	1336-1573
Azuchi Momoyama period	安土桃山時代	1573-1603
Edo period	江戸時代	1603 -1868
Early Edo period	江戸時代前期	1603-1690
Mid Edo period	江戸時代中期	1690-1780
(Genroku)	（元禄時代）	1688-1704
Late Edo period	江戸時代後期	1780-1852
Final Years	幕末	1853-1868
Meiji period	明治時代	1868-1912
Taisho period	大正時代	1912-1926
Showa period	昭和時代	1926-1989
Heisei period	平成時代	1989-2019
Reiwa period	令和時代	2019-

Notes: This table is written in agreement with the approximate AD year.

Part **1**

Professor Kohri's Travels
A Quest for Words

1 Japan's National Language, Japanese:
Knowing the Past and Looking to the Future

It is said that there are between 3,000 and 6,000 languages in the world. Japanese is predominantly spoken in Japan. Such an intensely monolingual environment, regarded as business as usual in Japan, is hard to find elsewhere in the world.

The protagonist in a current NHK historical drama is prominent industrialist, Eiichi Shibusawa,[1] whose life and ideas are currently attracting renewed attention. Shibusawa's portrait will be printed on the new 10,000-yen bill to be issued in the 2024 fiscal year. Japanese banknotes are printed with "10,000 yen" in both old-style Chinese characters and English.

In contrast, the front of Indian banknotes is in Hindi and English, the official national languages, and the reverse side is in 15 other languages, including Bengali, Tamil, and Assamese, clearly showing that India is a multilingual country. The largest linguistic group in Switzerland is German, but their regional Romance languages: French, Italian, and Romansh give them a total of four national languages. It is not unusual for a country to have more than one official language.

After the Meiji Restoration,[2] in which Shibusawa was active, there was a time when the Japanese language itself was considered a problem. Arinori Mori,[3] the first Minister of Education, considered the difficulty of the Japanese

---

[1] 渋沢栄一 Eiichi Shibusawa (1840-1931) was a Japanese businessman who served as an official in the Meiji government. He also was active in the establishment of schools and international exchange.

[2] 明治維新 *meijiishin*, or The Meiji Restoration (Meiji Revolution, Meiji Reform) refers to the modernization reforms that began in 1846. The shogunate-*han* system was overthrown to form a centralized government with the emperor in the highest position.

[3] 森有礼 Arinori Mori (1847-1889) was a Japanese politician, diplomat, and educator. He helped modernize the education system that led to the 6-3-3 primary-secondary school system. He served as the first Minister of Education.

language an obstacle to the opening of Japan to trade with Europe and the United States on an equal footing and advocated the adoption of English as the national language. Naoya Shiga,[4] one of Japan's great writers of the time, recommended French as the national language. If the abolition of the Japanese language had gone forward for political reasons, daily life would have been conducted in English for all official purposes, for example, school lessons and public conversations, while speaking with family members would have continued to be in the local common parlance such as the Tsugaru or Nanbu dialects in their respective regions.

What will happen to the Japanese language in the future? That depends on how we, the users, think and how we continue to employ the language. Knowing the past is connected to thinking about the present and looking to the future.

In the middle of the COVID-19 pandemic,[5] our movements were restricted, preventing a good deal of social interactions among people. Many of you may have come to realize through that experience that not only efficient and useful transactional conversations, but also less crucial, casual chit-chat and leisure time together are invaluable. While technological innovations and scientific information are of course important, knowledge of the humanities and sociology, including philosophy and ethics, is also essential to the discussion of the policies we all will follow.

Learning about familiar words and thinking about how we use them is anything but pointless. I am a researcher who is trying to elucidate the transitional journey of the Japanese language from the Kamakura and Muromachi periods to the Edo period based on old literary sources. Why don't you join me in this journey? Together we can consider the wonders of the language we unconsciously use every day.

---

[4] 志賀直哉 Naoya Shiga (1883-1971) was a Japanese novelist. He was awarded the Order of Cultural Merit. His works include "Dark Night's Passing" and "At Kinosaki."
[5] The term COVID-19 pandemic refers to the approximately three-year period from January 2020 to December 2022, when the novel COVID-19 infection occurred.

2 All about the Bento:
Taking Root in France and Becoming Part of Everyday Language

To avoid possibly spreading the COVID virus, I do not go out to eat these days. I eat a homemade bento, a lunch box that I bring every day and eat alone during my lunch break. Today's topic is the bento.

Bento, as a Japanese word, first appeared in literature during the Muromachi period. In "Shūekishō" (1477), a record of lectures on Confucian scriptures, there is an expression using bento that translates as "The right hand will do things conveniently," which gave way to the concept of bento as something "convenient" or "expedient." The Chinese characters used to write bento at the time were 便当 , and it was used in different contexts than the modern Japanese word bento.

In the "Nippojisho"[1] (1603), published by Jesuit missionaries for the purpose of learning Japanese, the meaning of "bento box" in addition to "abundance and sufficiency" is listed under the word entry "bentŏ." This tells us that the Chinese word bento, meaning "convenient," was being newly used in Japan in the early 17th century to mean "portable food" as well. The type of bento (弁当) I bring with me for lunch became popular in the Edo period, and is found in a quotation from "Haikai"[2] (1665), which means "By eating bento (弁当), we sow the seeds of the cherry blossom while enjoying cherry blossom viewing." This is a play on words, referring to cherry blossoms and "*makunouchi* bento," where *maku* carries both the meaning of "sowing flower seeds" as well as being part of the term *makunouchi*, used for a type of bento that contains a variety of ingredients.

---

[1] 日葡辞書 *nippojisho* (Japanese-Portuguese Dictionary, Portuguese: Vocabulario da Lingoa de Iapam, in modern Portuguese, Vocabulário da Língua do Japão) is a dictionary created by Portuguese missionaries.
[2] 俳諧 *haikai* is a form of *renga poetry*, a traditional poetry form consisting of regular 5-7-5 haiku poems followed by 7-7 side clauses created by multiple authors. This poetry was popular from the Muromachi period to the Edo period.

Not so long ago, when I was strolling in Paris, France, with my daughter, we found an interesting sign in a window on a street corner containing the word bento. While it originates from the Japanese, this is now an accepted French word. The meaning is a nutritious and convenient boxed lunch that features a variety of colorful ingredients and is beautifully packed.

A French dictionary published in 2013 has an entry for "bento," explaining it as "a meal you bring with you and eat during your lunch break (of Japanese origin)." While the editors make the decisions as to which words to include in a dictionary, the fact that this is listed is proof that bento has become an established, everyday word in France. Most words that have made their way from Japanese into French, such as *haiku* and *kimono*, were already included in an earlier dictionary, published in 1990, so bento seems to be a more recent acquisition.

From 便当 to 弁当 and then to "bento" in French, this is an exploratory journey through words. The bento culture that has been handed down in Japan since the Edo period is now attracting attention among 21st century Parisiennes. This is something to be proud of, isn't it?

3 On "Gentleness," and its Development into a Compliment

Dr. Shinsaku Fukuda, the 14th president of Hirosaki University, is a medical doctor and professor of gastroenterology who was appointed to the post at the onset of the COVID-19 pandemic. At this time of "social distancing," he declared, "I will create the most student-friendly university in Japan!" Despite the pandemic, Fukuda has shown strong leadership, including instituting a system-wide vaccination program at the university.

Hirosaki University has endeavored to create a comfortable environment where students can access everything from special learning opportunities and consultation to financial support. As part of both the faculty and the administration, I would like to take this opportunity on behalf of all my colleagues to express our sincere gratitude. I am involved in the university's daily education, so it is my hope that the students will never forget the kindness they have received in these trying times and grow into "gentle" people who are considerate of those around them.

The ancient word *yasashii* for "kind" has the same root as the verb *yasu* that means "to lose weight." Doesn't it seem a bit strange for "gentleness" and "weight loss" to have the same etymology? The word *omoiyasu* appears in the "Man'yōshū."[1] While we still use the expression "to **feel** thin" today. In the past the word "thin" was also used to describe thinness of one's body due to overconcern.

The poem in Vol. 5, the "Man'yōshū" is a poem of lamentation; "The world today is so depressing and painful that it makes me feel thin (*yasashi*), but I cannot fly away and escape, for I am not a bird." As seen in "*ah, hazukashikikana, **yasashikikana** (Oh, it's shameful and embarrassing)." from "Nihonryōiki,"[2] *yasashi* also expressed a feeling of "embarrassment" to the

---

[1] 万葉集 *man'yōshū*, or "The Man'yōshū" is the oldest collection of waka poetry in Japan, believed to be firmly established in the late Nara period.

extent that one feels emaciated.

The more one feels thin, the more one's thoughtfulness and shameful appearance come to be seen as attractive and beautiful by those around them, so they are praised. The word "*yasashi*," which expressed one's subjective feelings, gradually developed into a more objective term of praise in the aristocratic society of the Heian period. The other meaning of 易しい *yasashii* (easy) was newly introduced in the late Edo period.

Author Osamu Dazai,[3] who had a close relationship with our university, once wrote, in a letter to Yoshizō Kawamori:[4] "If you look closely at this character, you can see that it is a combination of the person radical (人) and *yū* (憂) which means 'to be worried,' so 'worried (憂) about people (人).' To be concerned about others, to be sensitive to their loneliness, sadness and pain, this is the essence of kindness and the best quality for a human being. Thus, the expression on the face of such a gentle person is always that of shyness." This interpretation is typical of Dazai, a shy man with a sensitive spirit, who also seems to have attached great importance to the word "gentleness."

---

[2] 日本霊異記 *nihonryōiki* (circa 810-824) is the oldest collection of Buddhist tales written and passed down from generation to generation during the early Heian period.
[3] 太宰治 Osamu Dazai (1909- 1948) was a popular Japanese novelist, born in Aomori. His real name was Shūji Tsushima.
[4] 河盛好蔵 Yoshizō Kawamori (1902-2000) was a Japanese French writer and critic. As a French literary scholar, he introduced moralist writings to Japan.

4 The Linguistics of Mystery:
Research is More Mysterious than Fiction

It's autumn, the season for reading, so I'll talk about books. The body of a person who had been strangled to death was found in the Kamata Railyard of the Japan National Railway. The victim's identity could not be determined making the investigation difficult. The detectives learned that a young man had been drinking with the victim the night before the incident. Using the word *kameda* in a Tohoku accent as one of the few clues, they pursued the investigation to find the man's whereabouts. Seichō Matsumoto's[1] "Inspector Imanishi Investigates" is a socially-conscious mystery in which the

Tohoku dialect is the key to solving the case. A real-life researcher at the National Institute for Japanese Language and Linguistics teaches the Theory of Dialectal Circumscription,[2] and a surprising background to the case is revealed.

In Seiichi Morimura's[3] "Proof of The Man," the key words are from a collection of poems by Yaso Saijō[4] and a straw hat. What is the mystery of "stouha" and "kiss

---

[1] 松本清張 Seichō Matsumoto (1909–1992) was a Japanese writer, who published more than 450 works including historical novels and non-fiction. He is credited with popularizing mystery novels in Japan.

[2] 方言周圏論 *hōgenshūkenron*, or Theory of Dialectal Circumscription is the idea that language is transmitted in concentric circles from the center of a culture.

[3] 森村誠一 Seiichi Morimura (1933-2023) was a Japanese novelist and author. His works include mystery novels, historical novels, and nonfiction.

[4] 西条八十 Yaso Saijō (1892-1970) was a Japanese poet, lyricist, and French literature scholar.

[5] It was first stated that "the r sound may be consciously pronounced weakly to conceal its Spanish origins," but this has been corrected on the advice of Berman.

me" uttered by the victim at the moment of his death? The investigation progresses with the testimony of a linguist who holds that "it is the way English learners sound when they try to approximate the sound 'r' weakly."[5] In this way, there are many cases in which the results of linguistic research can be used as scientific evidence, and this is a field in which we can contribute to society.

When I was in elementary school, I was crazy about mysteries. I immersed myself in them, forgetting to eat or sleep, and read works by Conan Doyle, Agatha Christie, and others. I was more interested in the sadness and unreasonableness of human society depicted in these books as a child than in the mystery tricks. I think I was exposed to the unknown world through books, and my sensitivity and imagination were nurtured.

Mystery novels are about enjoying the process of solving a mystery. You pile up evidence one by one, think logically, and get closer to the culprit. The path that one follows with excitement through the twists and turns to the solution, without knowing the conclusion, may be similar to research, which includes detailed observation of the phenomenon of language, gathering of evidence, and consideration of hypotheses.

Mysteries often lead to new ones. Insatiable curiosity and tenacity are the qualities required of researchers. As in mystery novels, research results will not be accepted unless the arguments are convincing to the reader. Nowadays, it is easy to obtain information and ideas for solutions. However, there is a sense of fulfillment and accomplishment that can only be obtained through the experience of agonizing over and being lost in one's own thoughts.

By the way, although it is generally referred to as the Tohoku dialect, there are delicate differences between Aomori and Akita, and between Tsugaru and Nanbu within Aomori Prefecture. Even in the Kansai dialect, Osaka and Kyoto are different, and Kobe has its own unique expressions. As for the identity of the Tohoku dialect in the aforementioned "Inspector Imanishi Investigates," it would be indecent to reveal the ending of a mystery novel. If you are interested, why don't you enjoy reading it on a long autumn night?

5 Science and the Japanese Language:
Learn in Your Native Language and Nurture Your Ability to Think

The Nobel Prize in Physics awarded to Syukuro Manabe has attracted attention for the excellence of his research results as well as his personality. It takes many years for basic research to be recognized, but even at the age of 90, I was struck by the way he continues to pursue research motivated by curiosity and inquisitiveness.

Hirosaki University has hosted academic lectures by world-class researchers. Anthropologist Juichi Yamagiwa spoke on "Human Society Becoming Monkeys." Nobel Prize winner in chemistry, Hideki Shirakawa gave us "Learning Science: Japanese and English." Nobel Prize winner in physics, Hiroshi Amano offered "LEDs Lighting the World." Japanese literature scholar, Robert Campbell presented "Japan as Seen Through Translation." Tasuku Honjo, Nobel Laureate in Physiology or Medicine spoke about "The Amazing Luck of Acquired Immunity." The lectures overflowed with information and inspiration. As we were able to experience the enthusiasm and fascinating words and actions of these top-notch professors, who talked about how their many failures and trial-and-error experiences led to new discoveries, we learned how good fortune lies beyond endless, steady efforts.

Hideki Shirakawa's talk was highly thought-provoking when considering elementary education in Japan. A foreign correspondent had asked him why so many Nobel Prize winners are Japanese, a high number among Asian countries, and Shirakawa said he had always been curious about the answer. The answer he came up with was, "It is because we were able to learn science in Japanese," Shirakawa

went on to say. In many other countries, science is taught in English, but in Japan, science is taught in Japanese. Language is not only a tool for communication, but also a tool for thinking. "The Japanese language is the basis of our thinking." English is necessary to communicate and interact with the world, but it is important to nurture the ability of Japanese people to think clearly in Japanese. Masahiko Fujiwara, an internationally renowned mathematician, also mentions the importance of Japanese language education in his book "The Mother Country is its Language," explaining that the ability of Japanese to use the Japanese language is the source of all intellectual activities, fostering logic and emotion.

The word, kagaku (科学), or science was newly created in Japan during the Meiji period. Western concepts, which had been rapidly introduced with the adoption of Western culture, had not existed in the minds of the Japanese until then. The word kagaku was first used in the "Tetsugakujii"[1] in 1881, but did not become popular until the end of the Meiji period. The word "chemistry" was translated as kagaku (化学) in 1860 by Kōmin Kawamoto.[2] Thanks to our predecessors in the Meiji Period who absorbed new ideas and institutions and struggled to convert them into Japanese, new words such as kagaku "science," kojin "individual," shakai "society," kaisha "company," ginkō "bank," tetsugaku "philosophy," jiyuu "freedom," and shugi "principles" were born and took root in the Japanese language.

[1] 哲学字彙 tetsugakujii, first published in 1881, is a Japanese glossary of academic terms edited by Tetsujirō Inoue and others. This book was responsible for the popularization of vocabulary, such as 哲学 tetsugaku, or philosophy, 科学 kagaku, or science, 形而上学 keijijyōgaku, or metaphysics, 普遍 fuhen, or universal, 意志 ishi, or will, 絶対 zettai , or absolute, or 契約 keiyaku, or contract, etc. The influence of these words extended not only to Japanese, but to Chinese and other languages.
[2] 川本幸民 Kōmin Kawamoto (1810-1871) was a physician and Dutch scholar during the late Edo and Meiji Restoration period.

6 Awareness of Dialect: An Important Cultural Heritage to Preserve

In Hirosaki, a survey shows that a high percentage of people have a contradictory attitude toward the Tsugaru dialect, saying, "I like the Tsugaru dialect, but I am ashamed of it." The dialectal words that students have taught me, such as *azumashii* (comfortable) and *shibareru* (biting cold) have an indescribable warmth and simplicity, and I have come to love them. I can see that diversity of language supports richness of expression and communication.

In my hometown of Nara, I have the impression that many people are indifferent to their local language. My father and sister commute to Osaka for work and school every day, and I used to go to college outside the prefecture. Those whose ancestors have lived in Nara for generations may have a strong attachment to their hometown, but Shiga Prefecture, being a bedroom town for Kyoto-Osaka, and Chiba Prefecture in the Tokyo metropolitan area exhibit similar survey results, showing a lack of interest in the language of the area where they live.

The word *hōgen* (dialect/regional language) is found in the early Heian period. "Tōdaijifujumonkō,"[1] already described, "These are our countries' *hōgen; Emishi* (an old term for Ainu), *Hida* (regional dialect), *Tōgoku* (Eastern dialect)," and regional differences in language have long been recognized. As the phrase "Eastern dialect" indicates, the language of the Kanto (Tokyo) region is now used as the standard language in Japan, but in the past, it was treated as one of the regional dialects. It can be read from literary sources that the language of the aristocratic society in Kansai, especially Kyoto, where

---

[1] 東大寺諷誦文稿 *tōdaijifujumonkō* is a collection of manuscripts preserved in Tōdaiji Temple, and was written in the early 9th century. It is a draft of Buddhist meetings, petitions, priests' oratories, and other ancient manuscripts.

[2] 源氏物語 *genjimonogatari*, or The Tale of Genji is a long fictional Japanese tale established in the mid-Heian period. It consists of 54 volumes. The author is Murasakishikibu.

the capital was located, was used as the standard. In "Genjimonogatari,"[2] Hitachinosuke[3] and his followers are looked down upon as "having an irascible Azuma voice (eastern dialect)." In "Konjakumonogatarishū,"[4] they are also derided as having "the sound of a crow cawing in the eastern lands." In "Heikemonogatari,"[5] Kiso Yoshinaka's[6] words and actions were also ridiculed, indicating that his local region was looked down upon.

Since the Meiji period, there was a long period in which dialects were not regarded as important, partly because standardized language was recommended in educational policy. However, as local dialects are being lost, they are now being recognized as an important cultural heritage that should be preserved. These dialects are destined to disappear gradually unless efforts are made to preserve them.

Hirosaki University has been conducting research on computer translation of Tsugaru dialect into standard Japanese using artificial intelligence (AI), and researchers are still struggling with the diversity of the Tsugaru dialect. In addition, students are actively learning from each other in classes dealing with dialects, and the classes are full of energy. For students from Sapporo and Tokyo where standard Japanese is used, the classes provide an opportunity to think about regional characteristics and historical development, leading to meaningful learning. Taking advantage of the characteristics of multi-disciplinary institution, the university's regional studies are not limited to dialects, but also focus on regional issues, aiming at developing multi-dimensional viewpoints and ways of thinking.

---

[3] 常陸介 Hitachinosuke is a fictional character in "The Tale of Genji."

[4] 今昔物語集 konjakumonogatarishū, or "Tales of Times Now Past" is a collection of stories established in the late Heian period. Author unknown.

[5] 平家物語 heikemonogatari, or "The Tale of Heike" is a Japanese military tale established in the Kamakura period. It depicts the rise and fall of the Heike samurai clan.

[6] 木曽義仲 Kiso Yoshinaka was a lord and military commander of Shinano Province region (now Nagano prefecture) in the late Heian period.

7 All about Soba:
Saving the World from Food Shortages

I was surprised to see "Herring soba" on the restaurant menu in Ajigasawa, Aomori. I had assumed that since it was a Kyoto specialty, it was only available at soba restaurants in Kyoto. Herring brought from Hokkaido via Obama, Wakasa, is boiled in sweetened soy sauce and topped on soba noodles. Considering the historical background of its origin in the *kitamaebune*[1] of the Edo period, it makes sense that it is served in Ajigasawa on the Japan Sea coast of the Tohoku region. Come to think of it, Osaka's specialty, salted kelp is also processed from Hokkaido kelp carried by *kitamaebune* vessels. So, a part of Kansai's food culture has been nurtured by the benefits of trade on the Japan Sea by the *kitamaebune* ships.

Buckwheat, on the other hand, has a long history in literature. In the "Shokunihongi,"[2] it was mentioned that Emperor Genshō recommended its cultivation in preparation for famine in 722, and in the Heian period dictionary "Wamyōruijūshō," it appears as *soba-mugi* and *kuro-mugi*. In the "Kokonchomonjyū" (1254), a collection of stories compiled by Narisue Tachibana, there is a story about Dōmyō Ajari,[3] who was served buckwheat by a mountain man and was impressed by the taste, saying, "Even birds do not eat buckwheat, but it is surprisingly delicious."

It seems that buckwheat was not yet a common food, but from the Kamakura period onward, there are scattered records of monks at Kōyasan[4]

---

[1] 北前船 *kitamaebune*, or northern-bound ships were merchant vessels plying the Sea of Japan from the Edo to the Meiji period. In addition to transportation, shipowners purchased goods and traded their cargo for profit.
[2] 続日本紀 *shokunihongi* is an imperial history book compiled in the early Heian period.
[3] 道明阿闍梨 *dōmyōajari*, or Abbot Dōmyō (974-1020) was a monk and poet of the mid-Heian period. He was a high priest and the abbot of Tennōji Temple, and one of the Thirty-six Poets of Japan.
[4] 高野山 *kōyasan* is a sacred site of Shingon Esoteric Buddhism opened by Kōbō Daishi at the beginning of the Heian period.

and Tōdaiji[5] temples making *soba-kai-mochi* (buckwheat cake). In the "Ujishūimonogatari,"[6] there is a story about a temple apprentice boy from Enryaku-ji Temple who is waiting for the *soba-kai-mochi* to be ready and looking forward to it, pretending to be asleep. Then, to his disappointment, others cared about him saying that it would be a pity to wake him up from his sleep, and he ended up not having an opportunity to eat it. It seems that back then, people used to eat it as *sobagaki*, or buckwheat paste kneaded with buckwheat flour and cooked in hot water.

It was not until the middle of the Edo period that buckwheat went from being an emergency food as a famine measure to an everyday food. Soba was supplied from Shinshu region and northern Kanto, where it was produced, and supported the diet of Edo, a city of one million people. Soba noodle shops flourished, and buckwheat noodles came to be eaten by the general public in the form of *soba-kiri*, buckwheat noodles. The custom of eating soba on New Year's Eve also spread, and it was described in "Honzōsho"[7] as being good for one's health.

Tsugaru soba is said to be made by kneading buckwheat flour in soybean soup and leaving it overnight, and the same method is described in "Sobazensho"[8] (1751). Tempura soba, one of my favorites appeared in "Morisadamankō,"[9] at the end of the Edo period together with the instructions to "add three or four deep-fried *shiba* shrimps." There are a variety of regional specialties, such as soba noodles served with spicy radish

---

[5] 東大寺 *tōdaiji* or Tōdaiji Temple is the head temple of the Kegon sect of Buddhism, located in Nara City. The main deity is Rushanabutsu, also known as the Great Buddha of Nara.

[6] 宇治拾遺物語 *ujishūimonogatari* is a collection of Japanese tales and stories estimated to have been written in the early Kamakura period. The editor is unknown.

[7] 本草書 *honzōsho* is a book on Chinese medicine produced mainly in China.

[8] 蕎麦全書 *sobazensho*, or The Book of Soba, is a book drafted by Nissinsha Yuukyoshi (real name unknown) in the Edo period. It is a detailed account of the situation of soba at that time, and is a valuable historical document for research on soba and the history of soba culture.

[9] 守貞漫稿 *morisadamankō* is a kind of encyclopedia describing customs and things in the three capitals (Kyoto, Osaka, and Edo) in the late Edo period. The author is Morisada Kitagawa (real name: Shōbei Kitagawa).

juice in Aizu, Fukushima Prefecture.

Not only found in Japan. Buckwheat galette is popular in France. Pizzocelli in northern Italy is a pasta made of buckwheat flour. Buckwheat flour is also eaten in Russia and China. In Germany, buckwheat flour is sometimes used as a binder for sausages. Buckwheat flour has been passed down from generation to generation in various ways to augment the food supply in various regions in the world.

8 *Kanpai*:
Chinese Origins, Taking Root in Japan

Kanpai, or toasts are a common part of year-end and New Year's parties. I am often requested to take the lead in giving a toast because of my position, but it's interesting to know that 乾杯 *kanpai* (toast) and 挨拶 *aisatsu* (greetings) are not words that have existed in Japan since ancient times, but rather they are words that originated in the Chinese language. It was only recently, after the Taisho period, that they have been written as 乾杯 *kanpai* and used in the sense of giving a congratulatory toast. Takitarō Minakami's[1] novel, "Inn at Osaka" (1925) says, "乾杯 *kanpai* in celebration of the closing of a business," while it seems that in earlier Japan, the kanji for "toast" was 勧める *susumeru*, (to recommend) used instead of 乾く *kawaku* (to dry.) The ancient Heian-period dictionaries "Irohajiruishō"[2] and "Ekirinbonsetsuyōshū"[3] (1597) use 勧杯 *kanpai* and do not list 乾杯 *kanpai* for a toast.

At a reception for an international academic conference held in China, a Chinese researcher said to me, "Prof. Kohri, *kanpai* is to dry up the cup, so please drink it in one gulp!" Not a drinker, I turned pale. In China, it literally means to dry the cup and drink it up. Nowadays, of course, we refrain from holding banquets to prevent the spread of infection, but in the past, in order not to make the party dull, I used to fill my cup with water and drink it down in a gulp pretending it was alcohol.

The word 挨拶 *aisatsu* (greetings) has become a part of the Japanese language, but it was originally a Buddhist term of Chinese origin. Both 挨 *ai* and 拶 *satsu* mean "to push," and the original meaning is "to push aside what is in front of you and start moving forward." In Zen Buddhism, the word

---

[1] 水上滝太郎 Takitarō Minakami (1887–1940) was a Japanese novelist and literary critic active during the Shōwa period.
[2] 色葉字類抄 *irohajiruishō* is an old Japanese dictionary compiled in the late Heian period using 47 iroha characters as the standard for word arrangement.
[3] 易林本節用集 *ekirinbonsetsuyōshū* is a Japanese dictionary compiled by Hirai Ekirin in 1597.

挨拶 *aisatsu* came to be used to "measure one's ability" and later changed to refer to the exchange of words.

There are many examples of Buddhist terms that entered Japan and took root, such as 蒲団 *futon* (mattress) and 旦那 *dan'na* (master). The reason that the Zen Buddhist term for "greeting" took hold is that it refers to the act of seriously confronting a person in order to estimate his or her ability. In other words, greetings are a way of measuring one's character and ability. If you know the original meaning, you will understand how important greetings are and how they cannot be neglected.

There have been cases in which the content of a politician's speech at a social gathering was discussed and became a problem, but, specifically, it is in the greeting that one's qualities and abilities are questioned and revealed. The recipient, the audience, must also have discerning eyes and ears to determine whether or not a person is genuine. A single greeting can earn respect or destroy credibility. I am not good at greeting people, but I would like to make an effort to at least improve my human qualities.

It is the end of the year. I would like to thank you for reading my articles and wish you all a happy New Year.

9 *Ozōni* in My Home:
Common Features in Dialect and Food Culture

Happy New Year! What kind of *zōni* did you enjoy on New Year's Day? The custom of celebrating the New Year with *zōni* originated in the late Muromachi period, as described in the "Nippojisho" (1603): 雑煮 *zōni* is a dish made from *mochi* (rice cakes) and vegetables served on New Year's Day. Stated in the "Ryōrimonogatari,"[1] (1643): "*Zōni* is prepared with miso or *sumashi* (clear soup). It goes well with rice cakes, tofu, sweet potatoes, radish, dried bonito shavings, dried abalone, rape flower leaves, and other ingredients." Whether the rice cake is round or square, in miso or *sumashi* soup, the cooking method and ingredients are unique to each region and household, and truly symbolizes the traditions and individuality of Japanese food culture.

My family has a simple *zōni*, a clear soup made of *kombu* (kelp) and bonito with chicken, fish loaf, *mitsuba* (Japanese chervil), and *yuzu* (a type of citrus fruit). We add toasted square slices of *mochi*. I inherited this Kanto style *zōni* from my mother who is from Tokyo. At my aunt's house in Nara (the main Kohri family household), taro, radish, carrot, tofu and chicken

---

[1] 料理物語 *ryōrimonogatari* is one of the representative cookbooks of the Edo period and consists of 20 chapters. The author is unknown. It is believed to be based on a book published in 1643, which compiled cooking methods passed down from generation to generation in the form of stories.

[2] 日本の食生活全集 (1993) *nihon'noshokuseikatsuzenshū* is a series of 50 volumes compiled through interviews with grandmothers; the books record the wisdom of dietary habits born from the climate and lifestyles of each prefecture, the ingredients of Japanese food that are about to disappear, and describe the unique food culture of each region.

are cooked with a combined paste of red and white miso, and a round rice cake is toasted and added in. This rice cake is dipped in sweet soybean flour when eaten. I was surprised at the combination of *zōni* and soybean flour. A university employee from Aomori told me that her family's *zōni* is made by simmering rice cakes in soy sauce-flavored broth that contains mostly root vegetables and *seri*, as well as dried tofu.

According to the "Nihon'noshokuseikatsuzenshū,"[2] there are two types of rice cakes: square rice cakes in Eastern Japan, from the Tokai region to the Kanto and Chubu regions, and round rice cakes in the Kinki, Chugoku, Shikoku, and Kyushu regions. Interestingly, the use of miso is limited to the Kinki region, Fukui, and Kagawa along with Tokushima in Shikoku, while the overwhelming majority of households, including Kanto, use *sumashi*. Noto in Ishikawa, Tottori, and Izumo in Shimane seem to have *zōni* with azuki beans. In terms of the shape of the rice cake, it seems that the boundary can be drawn between Toyama with square rice cakes and Ishikawa with round rice cakes on the Sea of Japan side, and between Mie with square rice cakes and Shiga with round rice cakes on the Pacific side. It is similar to the East-West dividing line of dialects with which I am more familiar. Food culture and language are both inherited and change over time, so there may be some common factors in the formation process.

At a friend's house, the wife's family observes the Kansai style on New Year's Day and then his family follows the Kanto tradition on 2nd day of the New Year, respecting both cultures. New Year's is a time to reflect upon one's family and hometown, while remembering the traditions and regional characteristics surrounding the festive bowls of *zōni*. I wish all of you a wonderful New Year with renewed spirit. Thank you for your continued support as we enter this new year.

10 *Umai* or *Oishi'i*:
Women's Flexible Ideas Become New Words

When you eat a tasty dish, do you say *umai* or *oishi'i*? Which one do you use without thinking to mean tasty or delicious? In Aomori, I was surprised when I encountered a female student who said *"umai!"* for "delicious." Elsewhere, this is considered male speech. But it seems that *umai* has been the standard form in Aomori for a long time.

According to a survey of dialects around 1965, "Nihongengochizu,"[1] *oishi'i* is used in the Kansai region and parts of Hokuriku, while *n'maka* is used in Kyushu, *n'me* in Iwate and Akita, and *umai* in Kanto and Aomori.

The recently published "Nihongogokan'nojiten,"[2] explains that *"oishi'i* used to be an elegant expression, meaning good taste, used predominantly by females; these days, however, men also use it frequently, and it has become an everyday word." A special expression used by some people becomes a common word once it is used by many people. This phenomenon can be seen in other cases as well, and is called "the law of diminishing deference," which states that the degree of deference decreases as an expression is used more and more. For example, *okāsan* (mother) was initially an expression of respect, but gradually became a common term of endearment.

The word *oishi'i* originated in the Kansai region, and it is assumed to have spread to the surrounding areas. In the Nippojisho, which reflects

---

[1] 日本言語地図 *nihongengochizu*, or The Linguistic Atlas of Japan is a publication by the National Institute for Japanese Language and Linguistics, called a linguistic map or dialect map, which shows the word forms and pronunciations of dialects in various regions of Japan. It was created for the purpose of clarifying the formation process of modern Japanese standard language and the history of various dialectal word forms using linguistic geographical methods. It is a basic resource on Japanese dialects that provides a panoramic view of the geographical distribution of dialects throughout Japan.

[2] 日本語語感の辞典 *nihongogokan'nojiten* (2010) is a dictionary focusing on word sense differences, or nuances, in Japanese language.

the language of the Muromachi period, the word *ishi'i* was listed as an item in the dictionary, and is described as "women's language." The "Onnaterakochōhōki," a book of manners written for women in the Edo period, also mentions that women used the term *ishi'yi*[3] instead of *umayi*. As the number of women using the word increased, it became less dignified, and *o-ishi'i* with the prefix "*o*" for politeness began to be used and took root. In "The Japanese-English Dictionary" compiled by Hepburn, who came to Japan as a missionary at the end of the Edo period, has the definition "delicious" listed under *oishi'i* and refers to it as "female speech." It is known that *ishi'i* and *oishi'i* were long recognized as women's words.

Men who wanted to use polite language also began to incorporate the expressions and spread them, and over the course of more than half a century, the number of users and the regions in which they were used expanded. Women created new words with flexible ideas, made them popular, and influenced the men around them. The word *oishi'i* is not the only word that has come to be used in this way. We can also see in the history of the Japanese language, the activities of women who have actively continued to pass on the baton of language.

---

[3] The sound "yi" in Japanese instead of "i" disappeared in the Meiji Period.

11 *Chizuko* or *Chidzuko*:
Different Pronunciations, Different Writing

One day last month, I received a bouquet of flowers saying "Happy Birthday!" I was so grateful to my co-workers who had paid attention to my birthday. I was born on a cold, snowy day, which is rare in the Kansai region. It is said that the first present you receive after being born into this world is your name, and the naming of 千寿子 *chizuko* reflects the wishes of my parents. In hiragana, my name is ちずこ *chizuko*, but it is sometimes mistaken for ちづこ *chidzuko*. Since some people do not differentiate the pronunciation among names like 千寿子, 千鶴子, and 千津子, pronouncing them *chizuko* or *chidzuko*, interchangeably, they may be confused unless they can see if the original kanji is *su* or *tsu*. Why are there two hiragana characters with interchangeable pronunciation?

The word 水 *mizu* (water) is written in hiragana as みず *mizu* (water) in modern Japanese dictionaries. In ancient times, however, it was written as みづ *midu*. In the Heian-period dictionary "Irohajiruishō," the Chinese character 水 is added with the pronunciation of *midu*, and 水 is also written as みづ *midu* in the "Ruijūmyōgishō"[1] established in 1251, the "Bunmeibonsetsuyōshū"[2] published in 1474, and the "Shogenjikōsetsuyōshū"[3] published in 1717.

Father Rodrigues was Portuguese. He came to Japan in 1577 and was so well-versed in the Japanese language that he edited a grammar book called "Nihongobunten," a Japanese Grammar Dictionary, for foreign missionaries. He described the language of the Japanese people of that time as sometimes pronouncing 水 as *mizu* and 参らず *mairazu* (not going) as *mairadu*. In other

---

[1] 類聚名義抄 *ruijūmyōgishō* is a Japanese dictionary for looking up Chinese characters that was established in the late Heian period.

[2] 文明本節用集 *bunmeibonsetsuyōshū* is a Japanese dictionary that is thought to have been established after the Muromachi period.

[3] 書言字考節用集 *shogenjikōsetsuyōshū* is a Japanese dictionary published in the Edo period.

words, he was saying that there were people who mispronounced *mizu* when it should have been pronounced *midu*, and people who mispronounced *mairadu* when *mairazu* was the correct pronunciation. This shows that the two different pronunciations of *zu* and *du* were becoming confused even at the time.

The word 水 was pronounced *midu* in ancient times, then *midzu*, and gradually changed to *mizu*, and became firmly established. According to documents from the Edo period, despite the change in pronunciation, kana notation did not follow suit, and the old form was retained. In addition to ズ *zu* and ヅ *dzu*, ジ *ji* and ヂ *dzi* have also followed a similar path. The difference in the hiragana characters means a difference in pronunciation. On the other hand, the hiragana characters for ゐ *yi* and ゑ *ye* in the ワ行 *wa-gyō* (*wa*-line) disappeared as the pronunciation was consolidated into the イ *i* and エ *e* in the ア行 *a-gyō* (*a*-line.) This is the result of the development of a national language policy after the Meiji period.

How do we accept the changing forms of the Japanese language? One part of the confusion caused by the fact that changes in pronunciation and writing did not occur simultaneously can be seen in the names Chizuko and Chidzuko.

12 Plum Blossom Viewing:
A Place for People to Flex Their Intellectual Muscles

It is the season for plum blossoms to bloom in various parts of Japan. The "Plum Blossom Viewing" in Vol. 5 of the "Man'yōshū" is the source of the original word for the new Japanese era name, *Reiwa* (令和), which began in 2019 with the enthronement of the new emperor. The name of the new period was composed by taking two Chinese characters from the poem which is entitled *The Preface to Thirty-two Plum Blossom Poems*. "On the thirteenth day of the first month of the year 730, a banquet was held at Ōtomono Tabito's[1] house. It was early spring, the moon and the air were clear (令) and the wind was calm (和), plum blossoms were in full bloom like the white powder of a beautiful woman dressed in front of a mirror, and fragrant herbs smelled like a sachet." It is said to have followed the structure and wording of the preface of early Tang poems such as Ō Gishi's[2] *Preface to the Poems Collected from the Orchid Pavilion*.

This is a scene in which officials posted to Dazaifu, a rural area far from Heijō-kyō, Nara's capital city, held a *hanami* (flower-viewing) banquet and recited *waka* poems. While cherry blossoms are now the most common *hanami* blossom, at that time, *ume* (Japanese plum) was an imported plant that could only be found in the gardens of aristocrats. Therefore, banquets held while viewing plum blossoms

---

[1] 大伴旅人 Ōtomono Tabito (665-731) was a Nara-period courtier, poet, and high-ranking official.
[2] 王羲之 Ō Gishi (Japanese pronunciation), or Wang Xizhi (Chinese pronunciation) (303–361) was a Chinese calligrapher, politician, and writer.

were high-caliber events. Around 726, Yamanoueno Okura[3] was assigned to Dazaifu as the provincial governor of Tsukushi, Kyushu, and a year or two later, Ōtomono Tabito was assigned to Dazaifu with his wife, Ōtomono Iratsume. Dazaifu's proximity to the Korean Peninsula and mainland China made it a cutting-edge location in terms of international and cultural exchange. These banquets were not just for drinking and plum blossom viewing but were also a test of intellectual culture and a battleground for academic and intellectual exchanges.

More than 160 plant species appear in the "Man'yōshū," which shows how familiar plants were to people in ancient times. According to "Man'yōnoibuki"[4] by Takashi Inukai,[5] the plant most frequently mentioned in the "Man'yōshū" is *hagi* (bush clover) which is in 140 poems, followed by *ume* (plum) in 118 poems, and surprisingly few cherry blossoms, only found in 40 poems. Plum blossoms are mentioned in spring *hanami*, and *hagi* in autumn *hanami*, and the fact that plum blossoms appear overwhelmingly more often than cherry blossoms suggests that in ancient times, the word "flower" was the plum blossom rather than the cherry blossom. However, according to Susumu Nakanishi[6] (who suggested the name of today's era, Reiwa), cherry blossoms may have been the representative flower even in those days, even though throughout the volumes of the "Man'yōshū" there are many selections focused entirely on plum blossoms.

As a resident of Hirosaki, I would also like to recommend cherry blossom viewing. In the Heian period, cherry blossoms appeared more frequently in the classics, with 12 mentions of plum blossoms compared to 29 cherry blossoms in the "Makuranosōshi"[7] and 34 of plum blossoms to 53 of cherry

---

[3] 山上憶良 Yamanoueno Okura (660-733) was an aristocrat, poet, and Japanese educator.
[4] 万葉のいぶき *man'yōnoibuki* (1983) is an essay collection of Man'yō poetry by Takashi Inukai.
[5] 犬養孝 Takashi Inukai (1907–1998) was a renowned Man'yō poetry researcher.
[6] 中西進 Susumu Nakanishi (1929-) is a prominent scholar of Man'yōshū poetry.
[7] 枕草子 *makuranosōshi* (circa 1000) is a classic work of Japanese literature established in the Heian period. It is a collection of about 300 essays written by Seishōnagon.

blossoms in the "Genjimonogatari" according to Tatsuo Miyajima's (ed.), "Classics Contrastive Word List," published by Kasama Shoin. In Aomori, the northernmost plum festival in Goshogawara is held around the end of April. We may be able to say that Aomori is a very luxurious area, where plum blossoms can be enjoyed at about the same time as the cherry blossoms.

13 Peach Festival:
Praying for the Growth of Children; the Warding off of Evil Spirits

March 3rd is *Hinamatsuri*, the Doll Festival, or Peach Festival. Peaches are a member of the rose family, like plums and cherries. An editor of the Toō Nippō Newspaper, to whom I am indebted for this series of articles, has a strong attachment to peaches, having named his son "Momotarō" (Peach Boy). Another young man from Aomori named Momotarō was in my seminar. One of my most memorable students, after graduation he became an elementary school teacher in Chiba and I attended his wedding. His parents named him after the kind-hearted but brave Momotarō from the old folktale.

Hinamatsuri is said to have originated in ancient China on the day of *Jōshisetsu*,[1] which is the first day of the snake in March that involves protection prayers. This custom came to Japan in the Heian period and was combined with *Hinaimatsuri*, a doll play festival for aristocratic girls that emerged in the Muromachi period. It was institutionalized as one of the *Gosekku*,[2] the Five Seasonal Festivals in the Edo period and gradually became commonplace.

There is a reason why peach blossoms are offered on the *Hinadan*, the doll platform where dolls are displayed. In ancient China, peaches were believed to have the spiritual power to ward off evil spirits, and "Shunjūsashiden"[3]

---

[1] 上巳節 *jōshisetsu*, on the first day of the snake in March in ancient China, was an event to pray for the prosperity of offspring, the exorcism of evil spirits, and good health at the turn of the season.

[2] 五節句 *gosekku*, or the Five Seasonal Festivals, refers to the turning points of the seasons as defined by the Chinese calendar during the Tang Dynasty. The five festivals were originally intended to be celebrated on days with odd numbers in the calendar, since the confluence of odd numbers (*yang*) was considered to be *yin*, events were held to purge evil spirits by drawing life force from seasonal plants, on January 7 (1/7), March 3 (3/3), May 5 (5/5), July 7 (7/7), and September 9 (9/9).

[3] 春秋左氏伝 *shunjūsashiden* is 30 volumes of notes on one of the five basic Confucian scriptures, *Shunjū*.

describes a bow made from a peach tree that warded off misfortune. In Japan, the story of the birth of the nation in "Kojiki"[4] tells of a scene in which Izanaki-no Mikoto (one of the first gods of Japan, the creator) throws peach seeds at his pursuers to drive them away as he flees from the land of the dead. Peach fruit and branches have long been used to ward off evil spirits. So, it was inevitable that Momotarō, the character in the old folktale who eliminates ogres, was born from a peach rather than another fruit.

Decorating with peach branches during the Girls' Festival was also probably meant to protect the girls from evil spirits and to pray for their safety. In China, peach trees are also considered to symbolize longevity and immortality. The legend of the Peach Garden, Utopia, in Tō Enmei's[5] "Tōkagenki," is well-known.

The story of Momotarō in "Akahon Momotarō,"[6] with notes added by Sanba Shikitei,[7] begins with the familiar "Once upon a time, an old man went to the mountain to collect twigs, while an old woman went to the river to wash clothes." The old woman picked up a peach that had floated down the river and took it home. The couple ate this peach, were rejuvenated and had a child. The couple named him Momotarō, and the son grew up to battle

---

[4] 古事記 kojiki (712) is the oldest extant history book of Japan that includes Japanese myths.

[5] 陶淵明 Tō Enmei (Japanese pronunciation), or Tao Yuanming (Chinese Pronunciation) (365-427) was a poet of the Six Dynasties Period in China.

[6] 赤本桃太郎 akahonmomotarō or Red Book Momotarō is an illustrated book that served as a written rather than an oral account.

[7] 式亭三馬 Sanba Shikitei (1776-1822) was a writer and ukiyo-e artist of the late Edo period.

ogres. Likewise, there was a related story in the Edo period that differed from the well-known prototype of the child being born from a large peach.

Plum and cherry blossoms are frequently mentioned in *waka* poems. On the other hand, peaches were often used in Chinese poetry. In "Genjimonogatari" and "Kokinwakashū," plum and cherry blossoms appear many times, but there is no mention of peach blossoms. Peaches seem to have played a different role than plums and cherry blossoms, which are objects of appreciation.

According to a survey of crops conducted by the Ministry of Agriculture, Forestry and Fisheries (2021), Yamanashi prefecture accounted for 31% of peach production, ranking first. Fukushima, Nagano, Yamagata, and Wakayama followed. It is surprising, though, that Okayama, which is famous for the original tale of Momotarō, was not in the top ranking.

14 Memories of Utō Shrine:
Yasukata, a Place with a Sad Story

It is again the season of graduation and other departures. At the end of March 1999, I landed at the still-snowy Aomori Airport full of anxiety and anticipation. I visited Utō Shrine[1] before starting my new life in Aomori, a place with which I had no connection. I solemnly pledged my determination to do my best in my duties that would start in April. I recall with nostalgia those events of 23 years ago, when I was worried, and am grateful for the fact that I have been able to live in good health and good spirits in this formerly unfamiliar snow country. It occurs to me that this may have been a benefit bestowed upon me during my first visit to Utō Shrine.

The main habitat of the *utō* bird[2] is isolated islands such as Daikokujima and Teuri-tō in Hokkaido, as well as Ashijima and Tsubakijima along the Sanriku Coast (Iwate-Miyagi Prefectures), where these creatures are rarely seen near humans. However, from the Muromachi period to the end of the Edo period, the *utō* was rather well-known as a bird with a sad story behind it.

In the *yōkyoku*,[3] the passage entitled "*Utō*," or the Bird of Knowledge, this bird is characterized as follows. Foolishly, this bird digs a hole in the ground to lay its eggs. The mother bird thinks the chicks are hidden and protected,

---

[1] 善知鳥神社 Utō Shrine is a shrine located in the center of today's Aomori City, which is said to be the birthplace of the city. At the time of the 19th Emperor Ingyō and when Utō Chūnagon Yasukata, one of the upper officials of the time, was convicted and exiled, he came to live in a place called Sotogahama in Mutsu Province. He eventually built a shrine dedicated to the three Munakata goddesses. Later, when Utō Chūnagon Yasukata died, an unfamiliar bird flew in from nowhere. When the mother bird chirped "*utō*," the baby bird chirped "*yasukata*" in response. It is said that the bird's name "*utō*" was derived from a transformation of Utō Chūnagon Yasukata's spirit.

[2] 善知鳥 *utō* or rhinoceros auklet is a seabird of the murrelet family (related to the puffin). Its total length is about 38 cm. The back, throat, and breast are black, and the belly is white. The beak is orange, and during the breeding season, the upper part of the beak lengthens.

but when a fisherman successfully imitates the birdcall "*utō*," the young bird responds with "*yasukata*." Soon the fisherman finds and captures the baby birds. The mother bird is so sad that she sprinkles tears of blood from the sky, looking for her children. The fisherman tries to escape wearing a straw raincoat and a hat, but the tears of blood continue to fall, and everything is dyed crimson red.

In the Muromachi Period, "Aromonogatari,"[4] contains a story that goes like this: "There is no treasure greater than a child. When the bird cries for her chicks, tears fall on a straw raincoat; it is the bird that cries *utō*, and the chicks that respond *yasukata*. I, too, shed tears on a crimson sleeve." The sorrowful feelings of the *utō* bird for her chick resonated in the hearts of the people and spread far and wide. The old *utai* song goes, "There's this bird in Mutsu, around the outer beach, and the sound of the crying bird is '*utōyasukata*.'" This is from an old poem found in the "Yōkyokushūyōshū."[5] In other songs like "Aromonogatari," the mother calls *utō* and the chick responds *yasukata*, but it's interesting to find that in this old song, the bird herself is said to call out *utōyasukata*.

Nonetheless, it seems that not only *utō* but also *utōyaskata* was commonly used as the name of this bird. In a dictionary from the Muromachi period, "Unpoirohashū" lists 善知鳥悪知鳥 *utōyasukata*, 有藤安方 *utōyasukata*, and 虚八姿 *utōyasukata* as bird names, while *utō* and *yasukata* are listed in the "Nippojisho" dictionary separately as bird names. In other words, there are three versions of this bird's name, *utō*, *yasukata*, and *utōyasukata*, all indicating the way they sing as well as the name of the bird, so they must have been somehow associated with the place name, 安方 *yasukata*.

The *Utō* in classical literature was a symbol of sorrow. For me, however, *Utō*

---

[3] 謡曲 *yōkyoku* or *utai* are ways to recite Noh lyrics, equivalent to a script in theater. Originally called 謡 *utai* (chants), it has also been called *yōkyoku* since Taisho/early Showa.

[4] 鴉鷺物語 *aromonogatari* is a war story in which birds are anthropomorphized.

[5] 謡曲拾葉集 *yōkyokushūyōshū* is a commentary on the *yōkyoku* chants of the Edo period.

is the first shrine I visited in Aomori, and I hold fond memories of the shrine that encouraged me to start my life anew.

15 The Wonder of *Sakuramochi*:
Aomori is Generous; It Offers Two Types of *Sakuramochi*

The cherry blossoms are in full bloom. By the way, did you know that the ingredients and shape of *sakuramochi*,[1] or cherry-blossom rice cake, vary depending on the region?

According to Japan's largest dictionary, "Nihonkokugodaijiten,"[2] to which I contributed as a writer and editor, describes *sakuramochi* as "a sweet made by dissolving flour in water and baking it thinly, rolling sweet bean paste in a thin, baked skin, and wrapping it in salted cherry leaves." What's that? This is different from the *sakuramochi* I have been familiar with since I was a child! The dictionary adds, "Sometimes glutinous rice is used instead of wheat flour." I was astonished at the explanation that the *sakuramochi* covered with glutinous rice in the pink color of cherry blossoms that I had in mind was a alternate form of *sakuramochi*.

I went to my favorite Japanese confectionary, Koganezawa, near the university to check it out. To my surprise, I found *sakuramochi* made with mochi rice, named *dōmyōji*, sitting neatly in the showcase. "Yes, that's right, the mainstream type is this *sakuramochi*, not some derivative product," I exclaimed to myself! I asked the owner of Koganezawa if this type of *sakuramochi* was common in Hirosaki. He replied, "We used to make and sell two types, but the glutinous rice based *dōmyōji* is more popular, so now we only sell this one. The other *wagashi* (Japanese sweets) shops in Hirosaki may sell two kinds, wheat flour and glutinous rice," he said.

The crêpe-shaped *sakuramochi* is said to have been invented by Shinroku Yamamoto who had his business in front of Chōmeiji Temple, a famous cherry blossom viewing spot in Mukōjima, Edo, described in

---

[1] 桜餅 *sakuramochi* is a Japanese confectionery associated with cherry blossoms.

[2] 日本国語大辞典 *nihonkokugodaijiten* is the largest dictionary of the Japanese language, volumes 1-13, published by Shōgakukan.

"Edomeibutsushi"[3] as Chōmeiji *sakuramochi*. In one of the works of Robun Kanagaki[4] there is a description that goes, "the pleasant fragrance of *sakuramochi* at Yamamoto's sweets shop in front of Chōmeiji Temple" (1872). This crêpe-shaped *sakuramochi* has remained a specialty of Chōmeiji Temple ever since the Edo period. As if to compete with it, the Kansai-style *sakuramochi* made of glutinous rice, *dōmyōjiko*[5] powder, with sweet bean paste wrapped inside, was born in and spread throughout Western Japan.[6] It seems that the flour-type *sakuramochi* from the Chōmeiji Temple in Edo was the first to be invented, but I was born in the Kansai region and grew up not knowing of its existence until recently. In Aomori, both the Kanto and Kansai styles are accepted, and I admire the generosity towards both.

In Western Japan, Chugoku, Shikoku, Tokai, Hokuriku, and Kyushu, glutinous rice *sakuramochi* seems to be common. In a part of the San'in[7] region (western Tottori and eastern Shimane prefectures), the Kanto style, from Chōmeiji Temple, is said to be more popular. It makes me think about the history of *sakuramochi* and the wonder of regional differences as we begin to enjoy the long-awaited spring season.

---

[3] 江戸名物詩 *edomeibutsushi* (1836) is a collection of *kyōshi* poems by Baian Kinoshita. *Kyōshi* is a non-standard Chinese poem.
[4] 仮名垣魯文 Robun Kanagaki (1829-1894) was a playwright and newspaper reporter; his real name was Bunzō Nozaki. His work includes "Aguranabe."
[5] 道明寺粉 *dōmyōjiko* powder is made from glutinous rice. The glutinous rice is steamed and dried, and then crushed into coarse pieces.
[6] 西日本 *nishinihon* or Western Japan refers to one of the two major regions, Western Japan and Eastern Japan. Japan is usually divided into eight areas: Hokkaido, Tohoku, Kanto, Chubu, Kinki, Chugoku, Shikoku, and Kyushu.
[7] 山陰 *san'in* or San'in is the region of Western Honshu facing the Sea of Japan.

16 On the Occasion of a New Term:
The Word "New" Takes on a New Meaning

Hirosaki University's entrance ceremony was held on April 5, and classes started on April 11. April is the month when the university is filled with the most vitality and fresh air. Although the COVID-19 infection disaster is ongoing, I hope that each student will take appropriate measures, and with their innovative ideas, figure out ways to make university life more fulfilling and meaningful. It is a new term not only at universities but also at elementary, junior high, and high schools. Today, let's think about the word *atarashi'i* (new). When we look up the ancient word *atarashi*, which is related to the modern word *atarashi'i* we find that it has an unexpected meaning.

In the "Kojiki," there is a story about Susano'ono Mikoto[1] coming up to the high heavens and intervening in the land cultivated by his elder sister, Amaterasu Ōmikami,[2] behaving in an unmanageable manner. Amaterasu defends her younger brother, saying, "The footpaths between rice paddies are destroyed and the furrows are filled in. My dear brother must have done it because he thought the land was untouched (*atarashi*)." Her defense of her brother's deed can be interpreted to mean that she thought he probably felt it was wasteland that had been left untended. Therefore, *atarashi* expresses a feeling of regret that something is not being fully utilized.

In the Heian-period, "Genjimonogatari" in the *Umegae* Chapter, a sentence reads "The princess is in full bloom, and her appearance is untouched (*atarashi*) and lovely." This sentence means that the princess is too beautiful to be left as is. The *ata* in *atarashi* is related to *ataru* (hit) and it means to wish something excellent or splendid to be so, but as I examine the

---

[1] 素戔嗚尊 Susano'ono Mikoto is a male god that appears in Japanese myth depicted in "Kojiki."
[2] 天照大神 Amaterasu Ōmikami is a female god that governs the sun; she appears in a Japanese myth found in "Kojiki."

examples, the word refers not only to admiration but also to a feeling of regret when an object is not exhibiting its magnificence. The kanji for 惜しき *atarashiki* (regret) is used in a *waka* poem by Ōtomono Yakamochi[3] in the "Man'yōshū," so there is large gap between the ancient word あたらし *atarashi* and the modern meaning of the word 新しい *atarashi'i*.

There is another word あらたし *aratashi*. In the "Man'yōshū" in a poem about the New Year, "I hope that as the new (*aratashiki*) year begins, more and more good things will fall and accumulate like the first snowfall of the year." This usage has been linked to modern words like *aratamu* and *aratamaru* that means to renew or make new. Originally two different words, *atarashi* (new) and *aratashi* (regret) became confused during the Heian period, and *atarashi* gradually lost the meaning of "regret" and came to have only the "new" meaning. It can be said that *atarashi* did not shift directly to the modern word "new," but acquired a **new** meaning.

I hope the new semester will be a good chance for you to acquire something new!

---

[3] 大伴家持 Ōtomono Yakamochi (718-785) was a courtier and poet of the Nara period. He was the son of Ōtomono Tabito.

17 Greenery Day:
There Is More Than One Way to Refer to a Color

It will soon be Golden Week, and May 4 is Greenery Day. This is also called the season of fresh greenery, but it was not until the Heian period that the word *midori* (green) was recognized as a color word. Before that time, people in the ancient Man'yōshū period used only four words for color: 赤 *aka* (red), 黒 *kuro* (black), 白 *shiro* (white) and 青 *ao* (blue). In other words, many other colors were expressed using these words.

For example, there are still regions where the word *ao* is used to mean 黄色 *kiiro* (yellow), so in that dialect *ao* is yellow and blue. In the "Kadzunohōgenkō,"[1] in an attempt to correct the dialect, the author explains as follows: "To call *kiiro* (yellow) using *ao* (blue) is a sheer misuse of the word. It should be changed." However, this is not a misuse of the word, but rather the inheritance of an ancient term for yellow. Not only in Kadzuno, Akita, but also in Okinawa, Echigo,[2] Hida,[3] and other areas from north to south, we can confirm that the word "yellow" has been used for *ao* in many dialects.

Midori is another color name that became independent from *ao* (blue) in the Heian period. The word *midorigo* (infant) in the "Man'yōshū" means "immature child like a young sprout," but neither *kiiro* nor *midori* is used as a color in the "Man'yōshū." The color name *midori* gradually became popular, referring to a color like young leaves, while *ao* had been used until then for such colors. The "Makuranosōshi" of the Heian period says, "The sky is *midori* and misty," and "The fan is best when its rib is made of magnolia,

---

[1] 鹿角方言考 *kadzunohōgenkō* (1953) is a book written by Takehachirō Ōsato and it explains the regional language of the Kadzuno region of Akita prefecture.
[2] 越後 Echigo is one of Japan's ancient regional areas and refers to present-day Niigata Prefecture.
[3] 飛騨 Hida is another ancient region referring to the northern part of present-day Gifu Prefecture.

and its color should be *aka*, *murasaki* or *midori*." The word *midori* can be recognized here as a color word. Perhaps we do not perceive it as unnatural to have the expression *ao-shingō* (green traffic light) in contrast with *aka-shingō* (red signal) because *ao* originally encompassed *midori* (green).

We think of the rainbow as having seven colors (red, orange, yellow, green, blue, and violet), but this is the modern Japanese sense of color. If we return to the framework of the four kinds of colors of ancient times, there are only two colors, *aka* and *ao*. In the "Nihonryōiki," a rainbow is described as "a cloud having five colors," and it seems that people thought of the rainbow as having five colors. So, there is no consistency in the way people perceive and label colors.

In English-speaking countries, the rainbow has six colors. In Shona, one of the languages of Zimbabwe in southern Africa, the rainbow has three colors: blue, green plus yellow, and red plus purple. In Basa, one of the languages of Liberia in Western Africa, purple, blue, and green are collectively one color, and yellow, orange, and red are collectively one, making a total of two colors. It is interesting to see how different language handles the color "green." The world is a big place indeed!

18 Tsugaru-san (Mr. Tsugaru) in Sakaiminato, Tottori

I am currently conducting research, funded by a national scientific research grant, on documents and materials from the Edo period that remain in the San'in region. Although the San'in region is quite far from Tohoku in terms of distance, I feel a mysterious connection to this region. Do you remember my introduction of Seichō Matsumoto's "Inspector Imanishi Investigates" in Essay 4 (P.104), The Linguistics of Mystery? I withheld my answer about the suspect who spoke Tohoku dialect; I stated, "It spoils the mystery novel if one reveals the details." The dialect that was thought to be Tohoku dialect was actually *Izumoben*.[1] In some parts of the San'in region of Western Japan, words with similar characteristics to the Tohoku dialect exist, having spread here and there, like a spattering of words. The reason for the similarity is not known, but it is interesting.

I was on a business trip to Sakaiminato City, Tottori, continuing my literature research on the San'in region, the theme being Japan Sea Area Exchange. I was surprised to find a place name "Tsugaru[2]-san" in Sakaiminato, Tottori. Legend has it that sometime in the late Edo period, there was a shipwreck near Koshinozu village. A Tsugaru sailor (called *kako*, which meant "sailor" then) drowned and drifted to the shore in what is now known

---

[1] 出雲弁 *izumoben* or Izumo dialect is a dialect spoken in the Izumo region. Izumo is now a part of Shimane Prefecture.
[2] 津軽 Tsugaru is a family of samurai and nobles who ruled the Tsugaru region of present-day Aomori Prefecture from the end of the 16th century until the abolition of the *han* (clan) system in Aomori Prefecture. It is the name of both the clan and the region.

as Hana-machi. The local people buried him with great care, and when sick people visited his grave and asked for help, they mysteriously got better. The grave quickly became popular, and people from all over visited it. The person was called "Tsugaru-san" (Mr. Tsugaru) because he had come from Tsugaru. The gravesite is still located near Daiba Park. According to "The Sakaiminato City History, Vol. 1," the shrine that remains was built in the Edo period.

During the Edo period, Sakaiminato was a port of call for the *kitamaebune*, ships that carried goods from Hokkaido and Tohoku to the Kansai region along this important transit point. As if to serve as proof of the maritime exchange, the belief of the common people in the curative nature of the name "Tsugaru" took root in this corner of Sakaiminato. The people of Sakaiminato showed compassion for the Tsugaru man who lost his life far away from his hometown. The folklore that this Tsugaru man rewarded the kindness shown to him by helping the sick people of Sakaiminato city seems to convey the importance of caring for others without regard to profit or loss. The proverb, "Mercy is not for others; it goes around and does good for ourselves later" comes to mind.

According to "the Public Opinion Survey on the Japanese Language" conducted by the Agency for Cultural Affairs (2000, 2010), many people seemed not to understand the concept of good deeds, thinking that "showing kindness to others does not actually help the other person in the end." About 46% misunderstood this in both the 2000 and 2010 surveys. According to the results of the 2010 survey, the Northeast region had a lower percentage of correct answers (about 32%) and showed a higher percentage of incorrect answers (about 58%). The correct interpretation of the saying, that kindness to others benefits the benefactors themselves is only a hindsight-based opinion. We should be willing to give a helping hand to those in need without thinking about the consequences.

19 Rainy Season:
Tsuyu Is the Common Word Today

June has arrived. When I lived in Kansai, I used to feel depressed because of the high humidity and continuous rain during this season. In Aomori, however, it is neither hot nor cold, and there is not so much rain, making it a relatively pleasant time of the year. The kanji for 梅 *ume* or "plum" and 雨 *ame* or "rain" are written together and read as 梅雨 *tsuyu*.[1] Let's take a moment to think about the background of the common use of this word, which refers to a natural phenomenon unique to this time of the year.

The dialectal distribution of the word 梅雨 *tsuyu* in the "6th Linguistic Atlas of Japan," compiled by the National Institute for Japanese Language and Linguistics, reveals some interesting facts. A dialect survey conducted from 1955 to 1965 for the purpose of creating a language map shows the actual language used at that time. The *tsuyu* form was widely distributed in Western Japan, from the Kansai region to the Chugoku region. On the other hand, *nyūbai* was used from the Kanto area to the Southern Tohoku region. This is a phonetic reading of the Chinese characters 入梅 which is thought to have referred to the exact start of the rainy season.

In addition, the word *tsuiri* is found in the southern Ki'i Peninsula and the Tokai region, *naga(a)me* in Iwate, and *nagashi* in Shikoku and Kyushu. In Hokkaido, in addition to *tsuyu* and *nyūbai*, the unusual word form *zuri* can be found in some areas. It can be assumed that the *nagame* and *nagashi* forms, which are associated with the meaning of "long-lasting rain," and the *nyūbai* and *tsuiri* forms, which mean "the beginning of the rainy season," were gradually merged into the word *tsuyu*.

It is often thought that the standard Japanese is based on the language of

---

[1] Rainy season usually falls between June and July. There are various theories as to why the character for *ume* (plum) is used to describe it, but this is the time that certain plums ripen.

Tokyo and Kanto, but there are many examples of words from Kansai, where the capital was located up until the Edo period, spreading throughout the country in this way. *Tsuyu* has a surprisingly short history in the Kanto region, and can be said to be an example of an expression from Kansai extending its influence throughout Japan.

The words *tsuiri* and *tsuyu* can be found in literature as well. A dictionary from the Muromachi period "Ikyōshū"[2] mentions 霤 *tsuiri*, and there is 雪 *tsuyu*, in "Bunmeibonsetsuyōshū." In the "Ekirinbonsetsuyōshū" (1597), *tsuiri* is embedded in the kanji 霖 and 墜栗花 . The kanji 梅雨 was used for *tsuyu* in "Nihonsaijiki"[3] (1688), where it says "This month we have a long rain that we have named 梅雨 *tsuyu*." Also, 梅雨 *tsuyu* appears in the dictionary "Shogenjikōsetsuyōshū." It seems to have become common during the Edo period and later.

It seems that it is only in the last half century that the phenomenon of continuous rainfall, unique to this time of the year, referred to differently in different regions, has become a universal word for "rainy season." A common understanding of the term has developed throughout the country only recently.

---

[2] 伊京集 *Ikyōshū* is a Japanese dictionary from the Muromachi period.
[3] 日本歳時記 *nihonsaijiki* is a book compiled by the Confucian scholar Ekiken Kaibara that introduces Japanese folk customs and events by season.

20 Cherry Memorial Day and the Tsugaru Prize: The Charm of Dazai's Literature Never Fades

Today, June 19, is the birthday of writer Osamu Dazai and also the day when his death was confirmed. His memorial day is called *Ōtōki*[1] or Cherry Memorial Day. The writer's real name is Shūji Tsushima and he was a graduate of the former Hirosaki High School, the predecessor of Hirosaki University, and several places related to him exist on the university grounds. Dazai's autographed notebooks (for English and moral training subject) from his high school days are in the collection of the university library. A replication of one of his notebooks is on display at the University Archives, so please visit if you have a chance. You will be able to experience an interesting part of Dazai's youth through the notes and scribbles he made between classes.

Hirosaki University has established the "Osamu Dazai Memorial Tsugaru Award" in honor of Dazai's work "Tsugaru." It is a regional exploration essay contest for high school students, and the application guidelines are published on the university website. The contest is designed to be held in conjunction with the "Period for Inquiry-Based Cross-Disciplinary Study," a newly established high school curriculum found in the Curriculum Guidelines of the Japanese Education Ministry, and entries will be judged in the fields of "History, Culture, and Society," "Technology, Environment, and Food," and "Life, Health, and Education." We hope that many high school students will take up the challenge, and that the name "Tsugaru Prize" will spread throughout the country much like the "Cherry Memorial Day."

"Run! Melos" is the most familiar work of Dazai that everyone has most likely read. The work has been included in Japanese language textbooks for many years. Along with Sōseki Natsume's "Kokoro,"[2] Ōgai Mori's "Maihime,"[3] and Ryūnosuke Akutagawa's "Rashōmon,"[4] it has become a staple of Japanese

---

[1] 桜桃忌 *Ōtōki*, or Cherry Memorial Day is Osamu Dazai's memorial day, which derives from his last short novel, "Ōtō" or "Cherries."

language textbooks. The number of works by great writers included in textbooks has not changed over the years, but it is noteworthy that a wide variety of works have been adopted from Dazai's works, including "Run! Melos" as well as "Fugakuhyakkei,"[5] "Joseito,"[5] "Hazakuratomateki,"[5] "Suzume,"[5] "Tokatonton,"[5] "Matsu,"[5] "Suisen,"[5] and "Chikukendan."[5] This is proof that the appeal and value of these works in the field of education is still alive today.

Critic Katsuichiro Kamei wrote, "If I were asked to choose only one of Dazai's literary works, I would pick 'Tsugaru.'[5] It is a perfect elucidation of Dazai's work, 'Bannen,'[5] and at the same time, it is a prophecy of 'Ningenshikkaku'[5] and 'Shayō.'[5] It is a work that connects the early and late periods of Dazai's life, and can be said to be the greatest key to understanding Dazai's literature." (Shinchōsha, "Dazai Osamu Collection, Vol. 2, Commentary"). "Tsugaru" is a novel disguised as a record of the culture and geography of a province, but it can also be read as an essay, a reportage, a travelogue, and an excellent regional theory.

As I go on to write this article, I find myself to wanting to read Dazai's novels again.

---

[2] こころ "Kokoro" is a mid-length novel published in 1914, which is representative of Sōseki Natsume's later years.
[3] 舞姫 *maihime*, or "The Dancing Girl," is a short novel published in 1890 by Ōgai Mori.
[4] 羅生門 "Rashōmon" is a short novel published in 1917 by Ryūnosuke Akutagawa, based on a tale from the "Konjakumonogatarishū."
[5] All these novels are works written by Osamu Dazai.

21 *Tanabata*, and Why It Is Also about Wishing for Better Calligraphy Skills

Tanabata will soon be upon us. Annual events are important in people's daily lives as they remind us of the seasons, but they have not necessarily been handed down in their original forms. The traditions have been passed on through time and social demands, while gradually being assigned new roles.

The Chronicle of the Six Dynasties Period in China, "Keisosaijiki,"[1] tells the legend of the stars, *Orihime* (Weaver Girl; Vega) and *Kengyū* (Cowherd; Altair). The couple meets only once a year, and the book describes an important event taking place on that day called *Kikkōden*, July 7, which involves wishing for improved skillfulness in the art of making things. There was a ceremony that involved offering wine, gourds, and fruits on an altar in the garden, asking the Cowherd and the Weaver Girl to improve their sewing skills by threading needles for them. The Chinese legend of *Tanabata* seems to have been introduced to Japan early on, and the "Man'yōshū" contains more than 130 *waka* poems about *Tanabata*.

In the Nara period, the ritual of *Kikkōden*, in which the two stars, *Kengyū* and *Orihime* were enshrined for the night at the Imperial Court on July 7, was recorded as a seasonal event. During the Heian period, it was passed down as a ceremonial rite of the nobility, and celebrating it was considered an elegant custom. In the Edo period, it was incorporated into samurai family events and gradually spread to the general public.

The picture book "Amanogawa," from Kanō Bunko[2] collection (Tohoku University), depicts how people in the Edo period celebrated the *Tanabata* Festival. Kimonos, thread, and *koto* (Japanese harps) are offered on an altar

---

[1] 荊楚歳時記 *keisosaijiki* is a type of monthly chronicle describing annual events in Central China written during the 6th and 7th centuries.
[2] 狩野文庫 *kanōbunko* is a collection of approximately 108,000 old books collected by Kōkichi Kanō (1865-1942), a famous thinker of the Meiji period.

in the garden along with sake and gourds, and *tanzaku* (paper strips) are attached to bamboo branches. Even today, in some areas, there is still the custom of "lending kimono" called "*Tanabata* paper robes," in which weavers are lent kimono to make them to look like the god of weaving. It seems *Tanabata* customs were handed down to the common people for them to wish for improvement in work done with the hands, such as writing, playing the *koto* (Japanese harp), and sewing. *Tanzaku* on bamboo branches are still seen at *Tanabata* festivals. Nowadays, it is customary to write down one's wishes, but it was different in the past. According to "Tanabata Seigashō" (published around the Genroku period), it says "There is a custom to offer *waka* poems related to *Tanabata*, but children may not know which are the best poems, so this book was created to collect and introduce *waka* poems about *Tanabata*." As you can see, poetry was an essential element of the *Tanabata* festival in the past. While it was an event to wish to the stars to improve various skills, it also served as an opportunity for children to study *waka* poetry and practice calligraphy.

Tanabata spread from the aristocratic culture of Kyoto to the provinces and the common people in the Edo period, and its transformation into the type of event in which children could participate has energized the event, making the occasion an established part of ordinary people's lives.

22 The Foreign Loanword "Beer" and What Dutch Scholars Have Taught Us

It is midsummer and people long for cold beer. In modern Japanese, there are many loanwords like "beer" that are derived from other languages. Although they are often thought of simply as words replicating the meaning and form of the original word, it is sometimes not easy to clarify the etymology and background of some loanwords. Some familiar words come from surprising sources: *tabako* is a word that came from Portuguese (*tobacco*), and *ikura* (salmon roe) is a word that came from Russian (*ikra*).

The English word "beer" is used on cans and bottles of the beverage, and it is often misunderstood that the katakana word ビール *bīru* (beer) is also of English origin. In fact, it is a loanword from the Dutch word "bier." When the word for the beverage is used alone, it is written as ビール *bīru*, but when combined with the word "hall," it is written in katakana as ビヤホール *biyahōru* (beer hall) instead of *bīru*. When combined with the word

"garden," it becomes ビヤガーデン *biyagāden* (beer garden).   How strange! Why is this?

The word ビール *bīru* seems to have been introduced by the Dutch around 1609, when a Dutch trading post was established in Hirado, Nagasaki. In "Orandamondō"[1] written by a Dutch translator in 1724, saying, "A liquor

---

[1] 和蘭問答 (1724) *orandamondō* is a book written in the mid-Edo period by Ichibei Imamura and Gohei Namura, two Dutch correspondents (interpreters and commercial officers), using information they obtained from the original Dutch.

made from wheat named *bīru*, has no taste." The Dutch scholar Gentaku Ōtsuki's[2] "Ransetsubenwaku" (1799) says, "*bīru* helps digest food and drink after a meal," and Yukichi Fukuzawa[3] also wrote in "Seiyōishokujyū" (1867), "*bīru* is barley wine, and tastes bitter."

The knowledge and experiences of Dutch scholars were the starting point for the importation and establishment of the Dutch pronunciation of *bier* in Japan. As Japan's interaction with English-speaking countries increased, the influence of the English word beer became more prevalent. When combined with other loan words, various new compound words influenced by English pronunciation emerged. However, when combined with Japanese or Chinese words to form compound words, the original Dutch rendering of "*bīru*" has not been lost, as in 黒ビール *kurobīru* (black beer), ビール瓶 *bīrubin* (beer bottle), 缶ビール *kanbīru* (canned beer), and ビール工場 *bīrukōjō* (beer factory).

Here is an interesting question; why is the instrument used in barbershops to trim hair called a バリカン *barikan* in Japan? The English expression is "hair clippers" and the French word is "tondeuse," so it seems not to have originated from either English or French. The origin of the word *barikan* was unknown for a long time, but Kyōsuke Kindaichi[4] discovered that the first imported clippers were made by a company called Bariquand & Marre and the company name became the product name. This is a famous anecdote that illustrates the efforts and persistence of linguists and the wonders of the integration of foreign vocabulary into Japanese.

---

[2] 大槻玄沢 Gentaku Ōtsuki (1757-1827) was a Japanese-Dutch scholar, a disciple of Genpaku Sugita and Ryōtaku Maeno, famous for their translation "Kaitai Shinsho" (New Book of Anatomy) from the Dutch translation of "Ontleedkundige Tafelen."
[3] 福沢諭吉 Yukichi Fukuzawa (1835-1901) was a Japanese enlightenment philosopher and educator, the founder of Keio University.
[4] 金田一京助 Kyōsuke Kindaichi (1882-1971) was a Japanese linguist. He is famous for his research on the Ainu language and for his contributions to the editing of a Japanese language dictionary.

23 All about Fruit:
Using the Same Terms for Snacks and Confectioneries

The representative fruit of Aomori is the apple. There are also cherries in early summer, Tsugaru melons, pears such as the General Leclerc, and black currants. In fact, Aomori has the largest black currant harvest in Japan. I am fascinated by the abundance and tastiness of Aomori's fruits.

By the way, the word *kudamono* (fruit) is also used to refer to different things. The word *ku* is an archaic form of *ki* (tree), and *da* is the current *no* (of) particle added to *mono* (thing, person). This has the same word structure as *kedamono* (beast). Literally, *kudamono* means "fruit of a tree." This is confirmed in an ancient dictionary, "Wamyōshō"[1] (circa 934), which says "*Konomi* (fruit of a tree), in other words, *kudamono*." In the Heian period, not only nuts such as acorns and chestnuts, but also cucumbers and eggplants, which are technically "berries," and root vegetables such as lotus roots, were all considered *kudamono*. Berry fruits, in particular, everything with a thin wall of small seeds from cucumbers to strawberries seem to have been called *kusakudamono* (grass fruits) according to the "Jikyōshū"[2] (1245).

Not limited to plant-based foods, side dishes and snacks with sake have also been referred to as *kudamono*. A reference in "Kagerōnikki"[3] stated "I used the lid of the sake container as a small plate and served *kudamono* on it." Also, "*Sakana, sakana kudamono*" (snacks for sake) are found in "Ruijūmyōgishō." The term *kudamono* was also used to refer to 菓子 *kashi*, or

---

[1] 和名抄 *wamyōshō* is another name for *wamyōruijūshō*, which is a Chinese-Japanese dictionary of the mid-Heian period, in 10 and 20 volumes, written by Minamotono Shitagō.

[2] 字鏡集 *jikyōshū* (1245) is a Chinese-Japanese dictionary said to have been compiled by Sugawara no Tamenaga. There is a 7-volume and a 20-volume edition.

[3] 蜻蛉日記 *kagerōnikki* (circa 974) is the diary of the mother of Fujiwarano Michitsuna in 3 vols. The diary depicts the mother's emotional journey as she struggles with her unstable marriage to Fujiwarano Kaneie, and her love for her son, as well as her awakening to the world of art.

sweets for snacking, and appeared in "Myōgoki"[4] (1275): "What exactly is *kudamono*? It is written as 菓子 *kashi* in kanji."

It was around the middle of the Edo period that the word *kudamono*, which had previously referred to nuts, snacks, and confections, came to mean exclusively fruit, which is now the modern usage. The word *kashi*, which had been synonymous with *kudamono*, gradually became limited to the modern meaning of sweet confections like *manjū* (sweet buns). It appeared in exchanges with countries on the Asian continent and with the introduction of tea ceremony. *Mizugashi* was another way of saying *kudamono*. From the mid-Edo period onward, the meanings were divided into "fruit" and "confections." It can be said that the word *kudamono*, which has existed since ancient times, has survived while the meaning and objects referred to have changed.

The apple, the pride of Aomori, appears as *ringou* in "Wamyōshō." The Chinese readings of the word are *rin'kin* and *rin'gon*, the latter of which seems to have been evolved into *ringo* (apple). Strawberry appears as *ichibiko* in the ancient "Nihonshoki"[5] (720), but in the "Honzōwamyō,"[6] the strawberry appears as *ichigo*, just like the modern word. *Mikan* is written *miccan* in "Nippojisho" (1603) and seems to have been pronounced *mikkan* in the Muromachi period. Watermelon, a typical summer fruit, seems to have been introduced to Japan during the Nanbokuchō period. The Rinzai sect monk Gidō Shūshin (1325-1388) wrote a poem about a "watermelon"

---

[4] 名語記 *myōgoki* (1275) is an etymological dictionary, written by Kyōson, during the Kamakura period.
[5] 日本書紀 *nihonshoki* is the Japan's oldest imperial history book, written in 720.
[6] 本草和名 *honzōwamyō* (901-923) is a book on herbalism from the early Heian period.

西瓜 (*suika*) in his Chinese poetry collection "Kūgeshū." The background of this familiar *kudamono* is also interesting.

24 Appellation:
The Language of Inherited Caring

"I love you." In English, the speaker is always I (me) and the recipient is you (you), whether we are lovers, married couples, or parents and children. In French, "I" is "Je," and in Chinese, "I" is "*wo.*" In Japanese, however, when speaking to one's own children, one does not use "I" but refers to in the third person as "ママは *mamawa*"(your mom...), or "お父さんは *otōsanwa*" (your dad...) when saying something intimate like this. In school settings, it is common to address students with comments from an instructor as "先生 は *senseiwa*" (your teacher...). Self-designation in Japanese is not fixed as a single word like the "I" in English. Expressions are used that replace I with the person's role, i.e., mother or father when addressing a child or the position of teacher when talking to a student. Japanese speakers believe that it is possible to stay true to oneself, yet flexibly adopt a designation influenced by relationships with others and the surroundings. There are many variations of self-designations such as *watashi, watakushi, boku, ore, sessha,* and in Tsugaru dialect, *wa, ora,* and many other words that are used in actual conversation. They may be used differently depending on the relationship with the other person and the distance between the parties.

In Japan, when a couple has a baby, they begin to call each other *papa* or *otōsan* (father) and *mama* or *okāsan* (mother). The grandmother in the eyes of the baby is called お婆ちゃん *obāchan* (grandma) by her own children, even though she had been called *okāsan* until then. It transforms into a name that is seen from the point of view of the relationship between the baby and the elder. Unlike English, where the self is fixed, in Japanese the self as seen by others takes precedence.

These days, when a Japanese husband introduces his wife, he is more likely to call her not only 家内 *kanai* and 女房 *nyōbō* but also 妻 *tsuma*, 嫁 さん *yomesan*, and うちの奥さん *uchino okusan*. Technically, it should be considered a misuse to say 嫁 *yome* (wife) or 奥さん *okusan* (madam) to refer to one's own wife. Is it out of deference to one's wife that men use the honorific title "san," even if it makes her sound like a stranger? Or is it a subtle sense of distance? 女房 *nyōbō*[1] is a word that has been used since the Middle Ages to refer to a wife in an occupational sense. Until the middle of the Meiji period, 家内 *kanai* meant "home," as in 家内安全 *kanaian'zen*, (security for the home) but after the translation of the English word "home" to mean "household" was established, *kanai* took on the meaning of "wife." Some of my acquaintances call their wives *waifu* (wife), so the term for wife depends on who is speaking. Isn't it interesting?

It seems that Japanese is a language with a heavy emphasis on consideration for others, not only in terms of appellation, but also in terms of instantaneously judging the other person, the situation, and the psychological distance in a conversation. It is a wonder of language that we usually perform this unconsciously. How can we learn about the past, reconsider the present, and connect it to the future? I hope that you will think about the background of the Japanese language that has been handed down to us and continue to use it with care. Thank you very much for your support over the past year in this quest for words, a journey of language exploration.

---

[1] 女房 *nyōbō* refers originally to a live-in woman working in the imperial court who is given a *bō* (a cell), or a small room, in the palace.

Part **2**

Discovering the Wonder
of Language

1 Kyoto Dialect:
Dialect Speakers Feel Pride and Disdain

I was born and raised in the Kansai region, but when I came to Hirosaki University in Aomori, Tohoku, and began lecturing there, I was told by students that they were "thrilled to hear the real Kansai dialect (*Kansai-ben*)." It seems that the language made a much stronger impression on them than the content of the class. I tried my best to lecture in the "lingua franca," but... it didn't work out that way. People from Kansai often seem to be misunderstood as sounding arrogant because they will speak Kansai-ben anytime, anywhere.

Back in the Kamakura period, there were two famous monks, Nichiren[1] and Sengaku.[2] Both were from the Kanto region. Since the lingua franca at that time was the language of Kyoto, where the capital was, they spoke what is now considered a dialect. Nichiren admonished his disciples who

were training in Kyoto: "Do not speak with a Kyoto accent. It is better to speak the dialect of the countryside." He was so proud of his own language that he described the Kyoto dialect with the word *namaru* (a slightly negative term for speaking with an accent). Sengaku, on the other hand, excuses his inferiority complex by saying, "The lowly pronunciation of the Kanto dialect is the result of phonological changes." These two dialect

---

[1] 日蓮 Nichiren (1222-1282) was the founder of the new Nichiren school of Buddhism in the Kamakura period.
[2] 仙覚 Sengaku (1203-1272) was a scholarly monk of the Tendai school of Buddhism. He is famous for his commentary and research on the "Man'yōshū."

speakers had opposite feelings of pride and disdain.

Today, as a Kansai native, I seem to have a mixture of both, not just self-pride like Nichiren, nor just condescension like Sengaku. It is my own language that I took a hard look at for the first time when I came to Aomori. Have you ever found yourself suddenly aware of the role of dialects and standard language?

2 Japanese:
Japanese Has Few Speakers

"What language do you speak?" A silly question in Japan, where most people speak Japanese, but in Belgium, where both French and Dutch are spoken, it is one of the questions that are used in the census. There is even a German-speaking region near the eastern border.

It is said that there are between 3,000 and 6,000 languages in the world, of which Japan is a minority word group.

This is what happened to me when I had to visit a friend in Switzerland. My father, who had simply assumed that Chinese is spoken in China and Spanish in Spain, asked me with a straight face, "Is Swiss spoken in Switzerland?" He asked me with a serious look on his face.

Actually, there is no such thing as Swiss, but several languages are spoken. In Geneva, where many international organizations are located, French is spoken. However, nearly 70% of the population speaks German, and 10% speak Italian. If we add Romansh, which is a remnant of ancient Latin, to these four languages, they have four official languages.

Most European countries are connected to their neighbors. It is common to see road signs in which two or more languages are written side by side. With such language variety within a country, it must be difficult to lead a life in reality. In Japan, as long as you can speak Japanese, you don't have to worry even if you are not good at English. Good for you.

3 Kana Characters:
Save Time and Effort

In the past, kanji characters were called *mana* (真名), meaning "true characters," while hiragana and katakana were called *kana*, meaning "temporary characters." Kanji with many strokes are difficult to write in small spaces with a brush. In such cases, kana was devised to be used as a substitute or supplemental character; kana was born from this.

Hiragana is a character based on cursive, or collapsed, kanji. For example, あ (*a*) is derived from 安 *an*, い is from 以 (*i*) and う is from 宇 (*u*) which were gradually transformed from collapsed Chinese characters. Katakana, on the other hand, is the abbreviation of a part of a kanji character, such as the *kozatohen* radical of 阿 , the *ninben* or person radical of 伊 , and the *u-kanmuri* or roof radical of 宇 . These were very rational ideas that saved time and effort and were considered a good way to eliminate inconvenience. The earliest written text with kana included was the "Tōdaijifujumonkō," a draft of a Buddhist sermon, written in the early Heian period. Later, it began to spread among Buddhist monks.

Katakana was useful in the Buddhist world and in aristocratic society because of its practicality. Hiragana was favored by women for its soft, curved characters, and was incorporated into daily life through diaries and waka poems. The two types of kana used today have a long, rich history.

Kanji:
Semantic Representation and Preventing Misunderstanding

When written all in hiragana, "かれはかいしゃにはいらない " can be read as both "*karewa kaishani hairanai*"(he does not want to enter the firm), or "*karewa kaishaniwa iranai*" (he is not needed at the firm).[1] How would you interpret this sentence in Japanese? One who reads it as "he will not join the company" would think, "he did not choose a particular company and decided of his own volition where he should work." However, if one reads it as "he is not needed at the company," it would probably be associated with "a company employee who is being laid off." Thus, you can see that kanji play an important role in creating a sentence that is less likely to be   misunderstood.

Kanji are ideographic characters (ideograms) that express both pronunciation and meaning at the same time. Most of the world's writing is in phonograms that express only pronunciation, like the English alphabet. Hiragana and katakana also belong to this category. The Japanese language is a singular example of the mixed use of different types of characters. This can be attributed to the fact that, originally, there were no characters in Classical Japanese. At first, the language borrowed sounds and meanings from Chinese characters. Kana was improved so that it could be written easily, and it represented only the pronunciation. Over the years, these borrowed (sometimes altered) and domestic-type characters were merged into a mixed writing system.

During the Meiji period, the trend toward Westernization led to proposals to make English the official language. This was a movement to eliminate Chinese characters. I am relieved that this never actually happened.

---

[1] This happens because "は "can be pronounced either *ha*, or *wa* depending on the context.

5 *Namamekashi'i*:
Does the Idea of "Pure Beauty" Change through the Ages?

In the "Isemonogatari (or The Tales of Ise)," written in the Heian period, there is a story about a man who falls in love at first sight with a *"namameita* woman" and sends her a passionate love letter. When we asked students to imagine such a woman, what she would look like, they came up with the Kanō sisters, Naomi Kawashima, and Norika Fujiwara.[1] They seemed to think of "glamorous women" as older, sensual women.

In "Konjakumonogatari," the kanji 生 *nama* for *namamekashi* is part of the word. In fact, the *nama* in *namameku on'na* translates to "fresh" and refers to a woman in her natural state. This would be the opposite of a mature and sexy woman; in other words, a young and pure woman is the literal meaning of ***namamekuon'na***. In the "Nippojisho," written in 1603 by a Jesuit missionary for the purpose of learning Japanese, *namamekashi'i* is rendered as "being amiable and beautiful."

Even in this period, this expression was not limited to the aesthetic sense of "sexy and bewitching." Therefore, *namamekashi'i* equates to the modern idea of "beautiful." However, the essential impression has changed drastically from young, pure beauty to mature beauty. Consequently, the woman in the "Isemonogatari," mentioned at the beginning of this article, was very different from what our students today expect her to be.

---

[1] 叶姉妹・川島なお美・藤原紀香 Kanō Sisters, Naomi Kawashima, and Norika Fujiwara are Japanese TV personalities and actresses.

6 Isolated language? Japanese Is of Unknown Ancestry

"Your eyes resemble your father's; your mouth is like your mother's; I wonder who you resemble personality-wise?" You all are made up of the parts you inherited from your parents and the personality you've developed since birth. Language, too, in fact, can be classified in the same way we connect ourselves to ancestors and relatives by analyzing certain characteristics.

This is what the study of comparative linguistics encompasses; languages are classified into "language families" just like human families. English, French, German, and other languages belong to the Indo-European language family. Japanese, however, still has no clear kinship. Such languages as Japanese are lonely and isolated and are therefore also called "isolates." It is said that "Japanese is difficult," partly because there are no similar languages. In contrast to Japanese, which is rarely used outside of Japan, English, despite being from a similar type of island nation, has spread remarkably overseas.

Although English is called "the universal language," Chinese has the largest number of native speakers. Spanish is second, English is third, etc. Japanese speakers come in at number nine among **native** speakers, with more native speakers than German or French (exact numbers are constantly changing). Japanese has become one of the most popular languages in the world due to Japan's huge economic presence. It is interesting to consider how the Japanese language, which we use without thinking, is positioned in the world, isn't it?

7 Tatami:
French for "Tatami"

Tatami is a flooring material that has been an essential part of Japanese life since ancient times. The word is a noun derived from the verb "to fold." Unlike today's tatami, it referred to a type of mat that can be "folded."

In the Heian period, the interior of a *shindendzukuri*,[1] the name for the architectural style of residences of the nobility, had plain wooden floors in every room. Tatami mats were then spread out or placed when/where necessary. In the old days, tatami mats were used for both seating and bedding. Tatami was rolled out for use among the aristocracy from the Kamakura period to the Muromachi period, when the *shoindzukuri*[2] came into use. It was not until the mid-Edo period that the tatami used today became familiar to the public.

In fact, "tatami" has become a keyword to describe Japanese culture overseas. The neologism *"tatamiser"* in French refers to the adoption of the Japanese lifestyle in interior design. This has been reimported, and Japanese encyclopedias that explain contemporary terms list the foreign word *tatamiser*.

Tatami thus has played a role not only in the spread of Japanese culture overseas, but in its original home in Japan, where it has recently become less common. At times it was used for the dining room with a *zataku* (a table with short legs used while sitting on the floor). In some cases, it was used in

---

[1] 寝殿造り *shindendzukuri* is a housing style for aristocrats which was used through the middle of the Heian period. In this style, the main house is built in the center facing south, with east, west, or north residences that are connected by passageways called *watadono*.

[2] 書院造り *shoindzukuri* is a style of Japanese residence that was used from the Muromachi period to the early modern period. In contrast to *shindendzukuri*, it is a form of samurai residence in which the *shoin* is the center of the building, which signifies a living room that also serves as a study.

living rooms for family reunions and entertaining, and at other times in the bedroom when a futon was laid out. Tatami mats suit the small living area in Japan, maximizing space, and have become an integral part of the Japanese way of life. It is a cultural phenomenon of which we can all be very proud.

Kimono and Clothing:
The Meaning Changes with Fashion

The Japanese kimono is already a term used in English today. This was largely due to the influence of Western civilization during the Meiji era that the word came to refer to what we know as a kimono.

In the Edo period, "Katakoto," a book on the study of modern language stated, "The clothing worn at home is called a kimono." The word kimono, however, originally referred to all clothing. The first edition of the Japanese-English dictionary, Hepburn's "Waeigorinshūsei,"[1] contained the words kimono and *fuku* (clothes) in its first edition in 1867, but *yōfuku* (western clothes) appeared in the third edition published nineteen years later. From this it can be inferred that the Western lifestyle took root during this period.

Both *fuku* and kimono were generic terms for clothing. However, as more and more people began to wear western-style clothing in their daily lives, *fuku* came to refer only to Western-style clothing. In Shimei Futabatei's[2] novel "Ukigumo," we find a sentence that says, "The man changed into a kimono and folded the *fuku* he had taken off." Kimono gradually came to be used exclusively for traditional Japanese clothing, and the relationship between *fuku* and kimono changed.

Just as the word "mode," which describes a fashion trend, is always about clothing in Japan, words related to clothing seem to be easily influenced by social conditions. In other words, it can be said that such words are adaptable and are quick to reflect the times.

---

[1] 和英語林集成 *waeigorinshūsei* is the first English-Japanese dictionary compiled by American missionary and physician, James Curtis Hepburn (1815-1911).

[2] 二葉亭四迷 Shimei Futabatei (1864-1909) was a Japanese novelist and translator of the Meiji era. In addition to his novel "Ukigumo," he is the author of the critique "Shōsetsu Sōron".

9 Futon:
How it Changed from Meaning a Type of Seat

Futon bedding is a familiar concept for Japanese people. The word 蒲団 *futon* at its inception, used to consist of the characters 蒲 meaning the plant *gama*[1] and 団 meaning "round," as in 団子- *dango* (dumpling). This is why, futon in olden days must have been round in shape.

The character combination 蒲団, which came to Japan along with Zen Buddhism in the Kamakura period, was pronounced "futon" in the *tōsō'on*.[2] "Shōbōgenzō," written by Dōgen,[3] the founder of the Sōtō sect of Zen Buddhism, states, "In teaching zazen, one should wear a *kesa* (Priest's robe) and use a futon." The word futon refers to a round rug woven from *gama* that is set down to sit on during zazen. Later, the usage changed from a type of seat to bedding.

It was during the Edo period that this change in meaning occurred. The futon was also a barometer of the popularity of professional prostitutes. They would beg their customers to give them a futon as a gift. There is an amusing story in the Edo *senryū*,[4] "I agreed to give her a *mitsubuton*[5] (a three- layered futon), but never heard from her again."

---

[1] 蒲 *gama*, or *Typha latifolia*, better known as broadleaf cattail, the leaves of which have been woven together to make a mat or a rug; the Chinese character means "grass that grows near water."

[2] 唐宋音 *tōsō'on* is one of the ways to read Chinese characters phonetically, which was introduced after the Kamakura period, influenced by the sounds of the late Ming and early Qing dynasties in China.

[3] 道元 Dōgen (1200-1253) was a Zen monk of the early Kamakura period who founded the Sōtō sect of Zen Buddhism. His "Shōbōgenzō" influenced later thinkers.

[4] 川柳 *senryū* is a short-poem type of literature that emerged in the mid-Edo period, and was used to capture personal and world affairs, manners, through witty expressions of 17 syllables.

[5] 三つ布団 *mitsubuton* or a three-layered futon was used by prostitutes of the highest rank in the Edo period.

As the original meaning has been replaced by bedding, the material has changed, and it is no longer related to *gama*. Thus, the original meaning of "a woven rug made of *gama*" has been forgotten, and the new Chinese character for 布団 *futon* was created, most likely to increase readability.

10 Dan'na:
An Expression of Respect, Now and Then

"They used to say it's better to have a new tatami mat with your new (young) wife, but these days it's better to have a new kitchen with your new (young) husband." Etsuko Ichihara, an actress with a strong personality, shouts this in a TV commercial. It makes me laugh because it shows how women have a lot to say nowadays in family relationships.

The word *dan'na* comes from a Sanskrit term that was imported with Buddhism. The Chinese characters, read *dana*, mean "to give," as it does in Romance Languages. In the Heian period, the kanji 檀那 *dan'na* was used to refer to *fuse* (donation) given to temples and to *danka* (parishioners). It gradually expanded to mean "patron" or "employer" and became an everyday expression of respect to refer to one's superiors, and the alternate kanji characters 旦那 *dan'na* came to be used as well.

It was not until the middle of the Edo period that it became a term of endearment to refer to one's "husband," as in the modern usage. Gradually, the degree of respect included in the word diminished. Recently, reflecting a world in which women's social status has improved, *dan'na* also seems to exist as a friendly expression from the wife's side.

In the commercial I mentioned in the beginning, if the actress had used 主人 *shujin* (master) or 夫 *otto* (husband), which is used in more formal conversation, it would have totally ruined the atmosphere. So, word choice not only offers a different impression, but also reflects the speaker's awareness!

11 Onigiri, a Term Originating in Kansai

Onigiri, or the rice ball, is one of the best-selling products at convenience stores. Nowadays, it seems that those flavors we used to associate with Mom's home cooking are sold everywhere.

This convenient on-the-go food used to be called にぎり いひ *nigiri'ihi*. The rice grains stick together when you pick it up. In "Hitachifudoki," a book about the Hitachi region (now Ibaraki Prefecture), written around the Nara period, it says "*nigiri'ihi* is called Tsukuba Country" which was used as a *makurakotoba*[1] for Tsukuba, because *tsuku* means stick together.

The term いひ *ihi* (rice) was changed to *kowaihi*, and then to *meshi* (cooked rice) in the Kamakura and Muromachi periods. The word onigiri was also changed from *nigiri'ihi* to *nigirimeshi*. And then the word was shifted to onigiri by adding the polite prefix "o" to the shortened form *nigiri*.

Omusubi is another old word used by women in the Heian period. However, once the term onigiri appeared in the Kansai region, it replaced *omusubi* in popularity and spread throughout the country. However, in addition to *nigirimeshi*, other names, such as *nigirimanma* and *nin'ni* remain, depending

---

[1] 枕詞 *makurakotoba* or pillow words are used for rhetorical, or rhyming purposes, mainly in *waka* poetry to set the tone or add a certain emotional quality by placing a word in front of another for poetic purposes.
[2] The word for rice ball is "musubi" in Hawaii, the most popular one being Spam musubi.

on the region.

In the U.S., except for Hawaii,[2] it is called a rice ball. This is convenient Japanese on-the-go food. It would not be surprising if rice balls became more popular overseas in the future.

12 Technical Terms for the Imperial Court, *nyōbōkotoba*

Murasaki Shikibu, who wrote "Genjimonogatari," and Seishōnagon, and the author of "Makuranosōshi," were women active in the Heian period. They were high-ranking members of the the emperor's or retired emperor's palace and were called *nyōbō* (court ladies).

The everyday words they used were understood only in their own circles, such as *ohiya* for water and *onaka* for belly. These words are collectively called *nyōbōkotoba* (court lady terms). They were originally a type of jargon used by members of the same profession and therefore were "technical terms," so to speak.

For instance, *okazu*, which refers to side dishes, is one instance of this phenomenon. In those days, meals were divided into a number of small plates and placed on the serving table. *Okazu* means "a number of things served together," created by adding the polite prefix "*o*" to the word *kazu* (number).

In this way, the court ladies avoided the common direct expressions of their time. They came up with various euphemistic phrases. Gradually, these elegant, feminine expressions spread to the court nobility, the warrior class, and even to the general populace.

It is quite amazing that these words are still in use after more than a thousand years. We live in an era where lifestyles have completely changed. Nevertheless, the language invented by the women of the court is still a part of society today.

13 The Word *bijin* Historically Included Young Men, too!

Is there any woman who feels bad about being called a 美人 *bijin* (a beauty)? This term refers to a woman who is good-looking, but since it literally means beautiful "person," one would think it should be used for both men and women.

The kanji 美 *bi* denotes not only beautiful, but also "tasty, big, fine." In the Chinese classics, a wise person with talent and virtue is also a 美人 .

In Japan, the word is thought to refer to women, but a unique usage can be seen from the Muromachi to the Edo period. The "Shigakutaiseishō," an annotated collection of Chinese writings by Zen monks, written in Japan in the Muromachi period, states, "*bijin* means a beautiful woman in Chinese. Young children and young adults are not called *bijin*, like we do in Japan." It seems that *bijin* was also used for boys in those days in Japan.

In the Edo period, in a *kanazōshi*[1] book, "*Shin'yūki*,"[2] says, "My only son, Shigemitsu, is a *bijin* at the age of 14." Saikaku Ihara,[3] who wrote "Ukiyozōshi" during the Genroku period, also described a man as "**bijin no goshisoku**" (your handsome son) and "What is the name of your second son, the *bijin* (handsome) lad?" The word *bijin* seems to have been regularly used to refer to young men in that period.

Nowadays, *bijin* almost always refers to women. However, we should always bear in mind that a true beauty is not simply beautiful on the outside, but also on the inside, with talent and virtue, in the truest sense of the word.

---

[1] 仮名草子 *kanazōshi* is a general term for novels written in *kana* (Japanese phonetic alphabets) in the early Edo period, which is supposed to be a casual book.
[2] 心友記 *shin'yūki* (1643) explains the arts practiced by homosexuals of the time.
[3] 井原西鶴 Saikaku Ihara (1642-1693) was a novelist and *haikai* poet active in Osaka during the Edo period. His famous works include "The Life of Amorous Man" and "Nippon'eitaigura."

14 *Koi*, an Expression of Loneliness

"Love is blind" is an English saying meaning that love makes one lose one's sense of reason and discretion. In Japan, the phrase "***koinoichinen***" (once you have fallen in love you become desperate) is oftentimes seen in the Japanese art form *jōruri*[1] to describe the passionate aspects of 恋 *koi* (love).

Originally, however, the nuance of the word *koi* placed more emphasis on the emotional feature of "quiet sadness." In the "Man'yōshū," the word 孤悲 *kofi* (solitary sorrow) appears. It is an accurate reflection of the feelings of the people of the time. It refers to the loneliness and sadness experienced when the one you love is not right in front of you, or the longing for the one you miss.

This is not only about romantic love, but also about nature and natural scenery as the objects of love, the lonely and sad feelings that arise in one's heart when one cannot fulfill one's wish to be with the person or thing to which one is attracted. This was the original core meaning of *koi*.

Even Norinaga Moto'ori,[2] a scholar of Japanese studies in the late Edo period, said "There is no greater feeling of human compassion than *koi*." He was saying that love

---

[1] 浄瑠璃 *jōruri* is a type of Japanese classical drama. A cultural art form popular in the Edo period. Theatrical music in which the *tayū* (a singer) narrates the storylines using the shamisen as an accompaniment instrument.

[2] 本居宣長 Norinaga Moto'ori (1730-1801) was a Japanese scholar of *kokugaku* (the study of Japanese classical literature) and physician in the Edo period.

enriches people's emotions and is of great significance.

The thoughts of people in the past are hidden in 孤悲 *kofi* (solitary sorrow). Norinaga also supports this, claiming it is "essential to life." However, it seems that traditional Japanese *koi* was important to people, to have the spirituality to accept sorrow and look into one's own heart without losing one's reason and senses.

15 Gradual Vowel Changes and Picking the Best, *erisuguri*

To "choose the especially good ones from a selection" is えりすぐり *erisuguri* or よりすぐり *yorisuguri*. The dictionary does not show a difference in meaning between them. Which one do you use?

In Old Japanese, this was a compound word from *eru* (to select), which can be found as used in the late Heian historical work, "Eigamonogatari,"[1] which states, "The emperor selected (*erisuguri*) good land and made it his dominion." On the other hand, the word *yoru* did not originally mean "to choose."

A Portuguese-Japanese dictionary from the Muromachi period includes the word *yerivaqe*, (*eriwake*). At that time, the "e" in *eriwake* was closer to the pronunciation "*ye*." This gradually changed to "yo" and led to the よ *yo* pronunciation. This is how *yoru* eventually came to mean "choose." This type of change is called a "vowel shift," and often appears in Muromachi period words. In the *sekkyōjōruri* "Ogurihan'gan"[2] and other works popular in the Edo period, *yorisuguri* appears. Both forms were probably in use by that time.

Words change and change. In some cases, it is not possible to strictly stipulate which is correct. However, at this time, as an academic, I have consciously started to use the original form, *erisuguri*.

---

[1] 栄華物語 *eigamonogatari* was the first Japanese historical book written in *kana*.
[2] 説教浄瑠璃 小栗判官 *sekkyōjōruri ogurihan'gan* is a popular folk entertainment that became popular during the Edo period. Buddhist sermons were converted into songs and performed together with shamisen and puppet shows.

16 Do Flowers Laugh? The Relationship Between *saku* and *warau*

In kanji, there is often a *hen* (left radical) that represents the meaning/category and a *tsukuri* (right radical) that represents the sound, although this system is more complex as evidenced by 花 (flower) which appears in the next sentence. When writing 花が咲く *hanagasaku* (flowers bloom), the kanji 咲 has a "mouth" part on the left, but it does not seem to carry a meaning related to the mouth, does it? In fact, 咲 (bloom) is the

main character from which 笑 (laugh) was derived. In the past, 咲 had the meaning "to laugh" which is, in fact, related to one's mouth.

The Heian-period dictionary, "Ruijūmyōgishō" annotates 咲 with readings of "*warau, emu*" (laugh, smile) and so on. Indeed, in the "Konjakumonogatarishū," a collection of tales from the same period, the kanji 咲 (bloom) is used for 咲ふ *warau* (laugh). It seems that the usage of 咲 く meaning "flowers blooming" was established during the Edo period. The dictionary "Shogenjikōsetsuyōshū," created around that time, assigns the reading *saku* to the kanji 咲 .

This may be because using this kanji for "to laugh" was enough to express the Japanese tendency to laugh with subtlety, i.e., more of a blooming than an outburst. Or perhaps someone started using the kanji because they felt as if flowers, in opening up, were smiling quietly.

Kanji like 咲 that have a different meaning from the original idea imported from Chinese are called 国訓 *kokkun*[1] (Japanese reading) or 借訓 *shakkun*[2] (phonetic reading for existing Japanese words). For example, the kanji 鮎 is read as *ayu* meaning "sweetfish" in Japan, but it means a "catfish" *(namazu)* in China. Surprising, isn't it?

---

[1] 国訓 *kokkun* is the reading of a kanji in Japanese that does not conform to Chinese usage.

[2] 借訓 *shakkun* is a method of using Chinese characters phonetically, i.e. just for the sound, as seen in the "Man'yōshū," etc.

Blue, How the Meaning Keeps Shrinking

A depressed mood is sometimes described as feeling "blue." According to an encyclopedia of fashionable words and phrases, "blue," which was once used only to describe colors, has recently come to be used to describe feelings in Japan, as well. This is an example of the expansion of the meaning and usage of a word for color to express feelings.

On the other hand, an example of a narrowing of the range of meaning can be seen in the translation of the word 青 *ao* (blue). In Japanese, *ao* was a very important word. In ancient times, *ao* represented a wide range of colors, including those now called "green" and "gray." Originally, only four colors had independent names: *aka* (red,) *kuro* (black,) *shiro* (white,) and *ao* (blue). A variety of colors were expressed using only these words.

The word 緑子 *midorigo* is found in the "Many'ōshū," and it means "a child, immature like a young sprout." This usage gradually became a word for "green," in its own right, referring to the color of young leaves. Since the Heian Period, using the imperial "Chokusenwakashū"[1] as an indicator, we can see that *ao* was being used less frequently, and being replaced by *midori*. The range originally included in the shades of *ao*, became independent words one by one. Even today, there are usages that do not strictly distinguish between *ao* and *midori*, as when the green of a traffic light is called *ao*. This seems like some sort of remnant of the influence of the perceptions and expressions of color in Old Japanese.

---

[1] 勅撰和歌集 *chokusenwakashū* was poetry compiled by each Imperial house. Twenty-one selected imperial *waka* anthologies were published over 534 years beginning with the "Kokinwakashū" (905) and ending with the "Shinshokukokinwakashū" (1439).

Furoshiki:
Started with Edo Period Rugs

When I got married, my parents made a *furoshiki*[1] for me with our family crest and my name dyed on it, along with a matching *fukusa*.[2] I wondered if I would ever use such things in this day and age, but I didn't want to make my parents unhappy, so, not daring to complain or ask for something more practical, I accepted them with the appropriate gratitude.

A *furoshiki* is a large square piece of cloth. The *furoshiki* became popular during the Genroku rule in the mid-Edo period. Today, a *furoshiki* is often used when people wear kimono and need to carry something, but, originally, it was part of daily life.

At first, it was used as a rug in the changing rooms of public bathhouses. It was also used to wrap clothes after undressing, or as a towel after taking a bath. The word *furoshiki* was derived from *furo* meaning "bath," and *shiku* meaning "to lay out," hence, to lay something out in a bathhouse. The emergence of the word *furoshiki* can be seen in a late Edo period dictionary called "Shogenjikōsetsuyōshū."

A *furoshiki* can be used to wrap objects of any shape. The ingenuity comes in the fact that it can then be nicely folded into a small portable shape. Moreover, it can be reused many times. It is much more environmentally-friendly than paper or plastic bags, which are thrown away rather quickly, when no longer needed.

Although my parents were so considerate to make a *furoshiki* especially for me, it is still in a drawer in my wardrobe and rarely used. However, in order not to waste resources, I am thinking about using this *furoshiki* again, knowing that it came to me filled with the sentiments of parental love.

---

[1] 風呂敷 a *furoshiki* is Japanese wrapping cloth for transporting various items.
[2] 袱紗 a *fukusa* is a small silk cloth for wiping tea ceremony utensils.

19 Dictionary:
The Many *migi Meanings*

The other day, I taught a model class at an elementary school affiliated with the university. I was very nervous because I had never taught in a primary, or even a secondary school setting before this. Despite my nerves, I think the experience helped foster an inquisitiveness toward language learning in the children.

The theme of this class was "Let's play with the dictionary." In this class students do not just look up words they do not know for a cursory understanding, but actually dive into reading the explanations. It is easy to believe that most dictionaries offer the same basic meanings, but when you compare them, you will find them to be surprisingly interesting reading.

Take the word *migi* (right), for example. One dictionary says, "the side on which most people hold chopsticks or pens," or "the direction to the east when facing north."

Another dictionary explains it as, "The direction to the west when standing facing south," or "The side of the road opposite to where cars are driven in Japan." Yet another says, "When you open this dictionary and read it, the side with the odd-numbered pages" and "When you face an analog clock, the side where the little hand points from one o'clock to five o'clock."

Each of these explanations has its own unique twist and character. Everyone understands the word "right," but it seems to be more difficult to explain it well. How would you describe it?

20 *Benjo*:
Now a Word that Leaves a Negative Impression

The Faculty of Education building is more than 40 years old. On the door of the Japanese-style toilet is the word 便所 *benjo* (toilet). The facilities in the School of Science and Technology building are newer, with the warm-water spraying function and the signs on the doors are all pictograms to indicate gender.[1]

Toilets were called *kawaya* in the past. The Muromachi period dictionary "Kagakushū"[2] lists 河屋 *kawaya*, meaning "toilet," but based on the characters, it is literally, "river roof." The origin of the word *kawaya* seems to be that the shape of the legs of a person doing his/her business across a stream was thought to look like the roof of a building. In Zen temples, the outhouses to the east of the monks' monastery were called 東司 *tōsu*, while those to the west were called 西浄 *seijō*, and the ones to the north, 雪隠 *secchin*.

In the "Kōyōgunkan," a military story book written during the Warring States period, the spacious six-mat latrine used by Shingen Takeda is referred to as *gokanjo* (rest room), avoiding any direct words. The term *benjo* became popular after the Edo period, but earlier, euphemistic expressions were used.

Although the foreign term "toilet" is now a well-established new name; people have always sought to improve the image of this place. Although far from the main purpose of a visit, *keshōshitsu* (powder room) is such a term.

After all, it is just a toilet. However, the difference in labeling can impact a person's impression of a restroom, an indication perhaps of the power of words.

---

[1] As of 2023, the Hirosaki University's Faculty of Education building has been renovated. The toilets are now labeled with pictograms rather than the word *benjo*.
[2] 下学集 *kagakushū* is a Japanese dictionary from the Muromachi period.

21 Chirping: Regional Differences in Onomatopoeia—

In Japan, the sound dogs make is considered to be *"wan wan"*; in English, however, it is "bow wow." It is an interesting phenomenon that the sounds made by dogs in Japan, the U.K., and the U.S. are different; should they not sound the same? When humans express their perceptions using the sound system of their own language, animal talk comes out completely different.

Modern people in Japan probably think of the sparrow's chirping as *"chun-chun."* However, the dictionary "Myōgoki" from the Kamakura period mentions it this way: "sparrows call *shiwu shiwu*." The Edo period *haikai* book, "Fūzokumonzen" describes it differently: "The crows cry *kākā*, and the sparrows chirp *chīchī*."

In "Suzumenogakko (School for Sparrows)," a *shōka*[1] song, composed in the Taishō period, goes like this, right? *"Chī chī pappa, chī pappa*, the sparrow schoolteacher goes *chī pappa*, shaking a wand."

According to a dialect survey conducted by the National Institute for Japanese Language and Linguistics around 1955, *"chū-chū"* was used for sparrows in Kanto, Chubu, Shikoku, and Kyushu, while *"chun-chun"* was favored only in the Kinki area. The spread to other regions of this Kinki-style call may have been the result of avoiding the same sounds as that of a squeaking mouse.

We use onomatopoeia without thinking about it much, but in many cases, it was a long road to our current everyday expressions.

---

[1] 唱歌 *shōka*, or songs for school music classes were created by incorporating Western music for school music education. This name refers to music classes in the old school system, and the songs themselves were also called *shōka*.

22 Vocabulary:
Japanese is the Leader of the Pack

In French and English, if you learn 1,000 words, you can understand about 80% of daily conversation. It is said that with 5,000 words, you can understand more than 90%. In contrast, Japanese is only 60% comprehensible after learning 1,000 words. To understand more than 90%, you need 22,000 words. The common usage vocabulary of the Japanese language is indeed large.

One of the reasons for the large vocabulary is that the Japanese language has a structure that facilitates the creation of new words. In other words, people are able to take advantage of this and devise and create new words, molding existing words into fresh ones.

In recent years, the misuse of words in Japanese has often been regarded as a problem or even a disorder, perhaps in need of a cure. However, it is important to remember that, first and foremost, language is constantly changing. The Japanese language, more so than any other, has a long history of adding words by adopting them from other cultures.

For example, 愚痴る *guchiru* (complain) is a portmanteau of the Chinese noun 愚痴 *guchi* (complaint) and the Japanese verb する *suru* (do), therefore creating "to complain." Student expressions such as メモる *memoru* (to take notes) and サボる *saboru* (to skip school/work), now commonly used, originally came from the English "memo" and the French "sabotage."

There are also many Japanese-English words such as サラリーマン "salaryman" and コストダウン "cost down." There may be a difference of opinions as to whether this is viewed as a lack of linguistic awareness on the part of the Japanese people or as an example of Japanese ingenuity.[1]

---

[1] In Japanese linguistics, this is known as "The Principle of Total Availability." It means that the language allows any new import to become established as a word. Many other languages, French, for example, think of this as a kind of linguistic invasion. Years ago, the French intelligentsia actively rallied against their young people calling Friday night through Sunday, "le weekend," thinking they already had their own term, "fin de semaine" (end of the week). Those against this phenomenon referred to it as "Cocacolanisme." France was not alone in this sentiment. Wikipedia has a page on "Cocacolonization," which sounds suspiciously like "colonization." Other countries have worried that the U.S. with its strong media presence is bringing too many English terms through movies and such to small cultures struggling to maintain their identities.

23 The Word *kowai* Also Means "Strong Belief"?

In the famous story, Princess Kaguyahime, when the *mikado* (emperor), the ruler of the country, hears rumors of the princess's beauty, he sends a messenger to court her, but she insists on rejecting his offer. Her foster father, the bamboo cutter, *Taketorino'okina*, excuses Kaguyahime's reaction saying that his daughter is *kowai* (which now means "scary"). But was Kaguyahime really that scary?

Today, *kowai* means "terrifying, terrible" and expresses a sense of fear. However, the ancient word *kowashi* is rendered as 堅 (hard) or 固 (firm) in Japan's oldest Chinese character encyclopedia, "Shinsenjikyō,"[1] and the kanji for 強 (strong) is used for it in "Irohajiruishō." The history of this word is "hard" and "strong," adjectives used to describe the nature or the state of something.

The expression *kowai kami* (paper) also appears in the story entitled "Insect loving Princess" in the "Tsutsumichūnagonmonogatari,"[2] which is said to be the world's oldest collection of short stories. Here, the word *kowai* refers to "hard and stiff" paper. Back to Kaguyahime, it can also be interpreted as a young person being "stubborn," a description of her character, not an indication that Kaguyahime was a fearsome woman, but rather that she was expressing her strong beliefs.

When confronted with something solid and strong, a formidable opponent, for example, people develop a fear reaction. For this reason, after the Muromachi period, the word *kowai* also came to be used to express fright.

---

[1] 新撰字鏡 *shinsenjikyō* (circa 898-901) is Japan's oldest Chinese-Japanese dictionary, compiled in the Heian period.
[2] 堤中納言物語 *tsutsumichūnagonmonogatari* is Japan's oldest collection of short stories, established in the Heian Period. The editor is unknown.

24 Castella, Not Originally a Japanese Word

Castella is a confection, a kind of sponge cake, that is very familiar to the average Japanese. It looks and sounds like a Western confection, but these days it is sold exclusively at Japanese confectionery shops. Why is this?

The Portuguese introduced the recipe at the beginning of the Edo period. It was called "pão de Castela" (bread from the Kingdom of Castile). In an encyclopedia of the time, "Wakansansaizue,"[1] the entry is 加須底羅 pronounced *kasuteira* (castella).

Castella also seems to have been used in tea ceremony. The "Kaiki,"[2] a tea ceremony record from long ago, states "*kasutera* was steamed and served." In addition, the "Taikōki"[3] written in the early Edo period describes the spread of the confection in this way: "For some people who don't drink, *kasuteira*, *bōru* (Japanese cookies), and *kompeitō* (Japanese sugar candy) were served."

From Nagasaki to Kyoto and Osaka, as it spread throughout the country, the cake recipe was improved to suit the tastes of the people of the time. It has become a confection unique to Japan. This is why this Western-looking cake is sold in Japanese confectionery shops.

There are other words of Portuguese origin that have become familiar in

---

[1] 和漢三才図会 *wakansansaizue* is an encyclopedia compiled by Terashima Ryōan in the mid-Edo period.

[2] 槐記 *kaiki* was a diary written between 1724 and 1735 by Michiyasu Yamashina, a court physician (chief physician) for the Konoe family. It contains many descriptions of court culture and study, especially tea ceremony and flower arrangement.

[3] 太閤記 *taikōki* (1625) is a biographical story about Hideyoshi Toyotomi written by Hoan Oze. Hideyoshi Toyotomi (1537-1599) was a warlord, during the Warring States period, who was called Taikō (a regent) for his unification of Japan during the ongoing conflicts.

the Japanese language, and not recognized as foreign, perhaps because they are written in kanji. Actually, 煙草 *tabako* and 天婦羅 tempura are such loanwords.

25 Shedding a Bad Image, *hayate*

Many years have passed since the Tohoku Shinkansen line was extended to stop at Hachinohe, and Aomori City. These bullet trains that run between the Tokyo metropolitan area and the northeastern part of Japan have been given the nickname Hayate.[1] The word *hayate* is old; it has been in use since the Heian period.

The term originally meant *hayachi*, "a terrible, raging wind." The Chinese characters 暴風 (terrible storm) in the "Irohajiruishō," dictionary of the time, has the reading *hayachi*. This *hayachi* appears in Seishōnagon's "Makuranosōshi," in the "Horrible Things" section, indicating that the word was not considered favorable.

Later, *hayate*, with its altered phonetics, became established. The Muromachi period dictionary "Onkochishinsho"[2] wrote this stormy word with these characters: 疾風 *hayate* (gale), while the Edo period *haikai* book, "Kefukigusa" introduced the homonym 早手 *hayate* (fast thing), indicating that the word *hayate* was used to emphasize its speed. The word *hayate* changed from the idea of a "gale" to "fast," gradually shedding its negative image. From now on, I believe that a fresh image will emerge like a rushing wind, as this nickname for the Shinkansen takes root.

The word *hayate* has changed with the times. Words are greatly influenced by the thoughts and consciousness of the people who use them. Language is a living thing that is connected through people from the past, present, and future.

---

[1] As of 2023, the Tohoku Shinkansen was extended to Shin-Hakodate-Hokuto in Hokkaido, and the nickname "Hayate" was changed to "Hayabusa," which means a peregrine falcon, instead.

[2] 温故知新書 (1484) *onkochishinsho* is the oldest Japanese-language dictionary from the late Muromachi period, that used the order of fifty syllabaries (starting with *a*). Until then, dictionaries were in *iroha* syllabary order.

■ 執筆者紹介

郡　千寿子　Kohri Chizuko

弘前大学　理事・副学長。博士（文学）。1965年奈良市生まれ。
武庫川女子大学大学院文学研究科修了。同大助手を経て1999年弘前大学助教授、2010年教授、2016年から現職。全国大学国語国文学会役員のほか、青森県立高等学校魅力づくり検討会議議長、弘前市立図書館協議会委員長、青森テレビ放送番組審議会副委員長、弘前れんが倉庫美術館運営審議会委員など地域社会活動にも従事。編著書『真字本方丈記』（和泉書院）、『日本国語大辞典1～13巻』(小学館)、『日本語大事典　上下巻』(朝倉書店)、『日本語 文章・文体・表現事典』(朝倉書店)、『青森の文学世界』(弘前大学出版会)、『寺山修司という疑問符』(同)、『太宰へのまなざし』(同) など。専門は日本語学、語彙・表記史。

多田　恵実　Tada Megumi

弘前大学教育推進機構　准教授。1960年弘前市生れ。
青山学院大学英米文学科卒、学習院大学イギリス文学専攻博士前期課程修了、The University of Maryland, Asian Division, B.A. (Management・経営学士) 卒、IBM World Trade Asia Corporation 勤務を経て本学専任講師、2020年から現職。専門は英米文学、英語教育。

バーマン　シャーリー　ジョイ　Berman, Shari Joy

弘前大学医学部附属病院　特任准教授。1955年アメリカ合衆国生れ。
教師、トレーナー、翻訳家、作家。東京の企業や語学学校で教員研修を行う傍ら、東京外国語大学でも教鞭をとる。『考えて解く TOEIC® L&R TEST 実践演習』(成美堂)、『CD付き 正しく診断するための診療英会話』(ナツメ社) など。1986年有限会社ジャパンランゲージフォーラム（JLF）を設立。2022年ユダヤ教スピリチュアル・リーダーズ・インスティテュート（JSLI）よりラビとして叙階、2023年には JSLI より「アソシエート・ラビ」として任命、ニューヨークを拠点に宗教礼拝を指導している。

つちや　牧子　Tsuchiya Makiko

エディトリアルデザイナー。1961年東京都生れ。
武蔵野美術大学造形学部卒、弘前大学大学院教育学研究科修了。2000年造本装幀コンクール文部大臣賞『とんとんとんのこもりうた』(講談社／作・絵：いもと ようこ)。『げんき』(講談社) など育児月刊誌、実用書のデザインやイラストを主に手掛けてきた。弘前市在住。

コオリ先生のことば探求紀行
Professor Kohri's Travels: A Quest for Words

2024年3月25日　初版第1刷発行

著　者　　郡　千寿子　Kohri Chizuko
　　　　　多田　恵実　Tada Megumi
　　　　　バーマン　シャーリー　ジョイ　Berman, Shari Joy

イラスト・装丁・デザイン
　　　　　つちや　牧子（sekka Design）

発行所　弘前大学出版会　　**HUP**
　　　　　〒036-8560　青森県弘前市文京町1
　　　　　Tel. 0172-39-3168　Fax. 0172-39-3171

印刷・製本　小野印刷所

ISBN 978-4-910425-15-3